The Small Business Tax Guide

Crystal Stranger, EA

ISBN: **0692293043**
ISBN-13: **9780692293041**

DEDICATION

This book is dedicated to my daughter Synne. Having her inspired me to want to share the knowledge I have with others.

CONTENTS

ACKNOWLEDGMENTS

I am eternally grateful for the skills I learned from my parents- from my father the math abilities to understand financial problems, and from my mother the creativity to always ask "is there any other solution?"

"Over and over again courts have said that there is nothing sinister in so arranging one's affairs as to keep taxes as low as possible." - Judge Learned Hand

INTRODUCTION

I've always been surprised by how little good tax information and services are available to small business owners. There are lots of guides for personal tax and investment, but very little available to help those who have gotten just a bit more complicated as their businesses grow. This book is for those entrepreneurial spirits, to give you a background and understanding of the tax concepts that affect your ability to make- and keep- money.

This book is not intended as a catch all or do-it-yourself guide. And please don't misconstrue anything in here as legal advice- always consult with the appropriate lawyers or accountants before making financial decisions as these rules change frequently.

My intention here was to share more concepts and basic numbers so that forecasting can be done of what you may owe the following year. I've always liked to take that into consideration when making my own business and investment decisions, and found the information I need was spread across books, IRS regulations and contacting others in the field to hear opinions of what works in practice.

Tax preparation has some hard and fast rules, but there are many areas where what is customary and allowed runs contrary to any logic. In addition there are many grey areas where different preparers have varying comfort levels with regards to what in their opinion is within the spirit of the law.

Many concepts in this book are very simplified and the qualifications abbreviated. Why? I wanted to make this a readable book. And frankly, for most people outside of the accounting field reading about this subject is the great cure for insomnia. Each chapter could be expanded easily into a book of its own, and chapter 12, about state taxes, could become an encyclopedia set. But I wanted to give the information I look for to make decisions- what will it cost me to do this business idea. And this sort of handy reference guide for business decisions and thought about from that angle is something I've never run across.

So read on and I hope you enjoy. This book is not meant to be read in order. Please feel free to jump around from chapter to chapter as your needs see fit. Some of the information in here may feel a bit daunting at first, if you have questions I welcome your feedback, contact information will be listed at the back of the book. Wishing you success and prosperity in your business endeavors.

Chapter 1: THE WORLD OF TAX

Magically Disappearing Money

Once upon a time in a land not so far away a magical man waved his wand saying, "just give me your money and you will never pay tax again." With his magic wand he made your tax liability disappear- and your money disappeared along with it.

Making money and keeping the money you make should always be the priority, unfortunately this is an often overlooked concept in the tax field. This holistic view is a philosophy I want to share with you before we get into the details.

> *Tax Tip: All investment and spending decisions should make sense on a number of levels- tax savings being the icing on the cake.*

An old caveat of investing is: "it's not about how much money you make, but how much money you keep." That was how I got into the tax field in the first place.

I was a real estate investor in California during the start of the last boom. I had made some great investments- one time buying a property for $12,000 that I turned around a month later and sold a portion of it off for over $100,000, still leaving me with a rental house. I sold that land to a developer who was willing to play ball, and I could structure the deal any way I wanted tax-wise.

I went from one CPA to the next asking about complex tax strategies and nobody could answer my questions to tell me what my tax liability would be. This led to me entering study programs and becoming an Enrolled Agent (those little EA letters after my name I have to thank for this...) before I had found my answer.

So You Say...

Before we get into the details I want to mention another very important element of tax preparation- semantics. When you are planning your tax strategies it is very important to know that what you are doing is considered tax planning.

Be very careful to never talk in terms such as avoiding taxes, or looking for tax shelters. And avoid like the plague any advisor who will mention such things- they will get you into more trouble than they are worth.

This is the hallmark of the types of schemes that get investors huge fines for tax avoidance, and the con-men that prey on unsuspecting business owners are always lurking in the shadows with their "too good to be true" offers.

> *Tax Tip: Never say you are "avoiding" taxes. Always talk in terms of "tax planning" or you may get into trouble no matter how legal your tax strategies are.*

The truth is, there are a lot of great tax planning strategies, but no easy one that covers all situations. Tax code is full of grey areas, the more one learns and becomes an expert in the field the more it is obvious that nobody knows but a small portion of the tax code, including auditors. How aggressive you want to get into these grey areas are up to you.

Chapter 15 will cover these grey areas- return disclosed tax positions and foreign tax strategies. However, I will mention now that I would reserve those for only the situations where they are needed. The vast majority of small business returns I have reviewed coming from other preparers have room for legal improvement. Often with very basic mistakes such as not utilizing depreciation to the greatest benefit of the client, or leaving out expenses the client did not know were deductible and the preparer did not ask enough questions in the discovery process.

Do You Need a Tax Preparer?

This comes to the next issue, who really needs to hire a tax preparer? Many preparers may be outraged that I say this, but I'd say at least half of the taxpaying public does not receive value in hiring a tax accountant, aside from the feel-good handholding aspect. These are the backbone of America- W-2 wage earning, standard deduction taking, hard working Americans. With a good tax software even itemized deductions and education credits can be tackled by most. Earned income credit is the domain of H&R Block and other storefront chains who make their money off refund loans for taxpayers who get refundable credits of about half what they earned during the year.

But which taxpayers really benefit from hiring an accountant? In my opinion the following situations, and many more, are when having a professional will save you more than the fees you pay:

- Self-employment income. (Schedule C)
- More than one rental property. (Schedule E)
- Sale of real estate or business. (Form 8949)
- Cancellation of Debt. (Form 982)
- Partnerships, LLC, or Limited Partnership. (Form 1065)
- Corporation (1120 and 1120S)
- Foreign earned income exclusion. (Form 2555)
- Foreign corporation. (Form 5471)

Having someone to ask questions to (and hopefully they will give intelligent answers), is one of the greatest values of a good tax accountant. To be fully honest, I don't even like to fully prepare my own tax return without asking someone to review it- usually my dad who has been an accountant for forty-some years. He doesn't always find changes, but often asks questions that lead me to think of ways I could more clearly show something or ideas for tax planning in the future.

In addition, one of the biggest reasons to hire a professional is that they know when to say stop. Taking away too many deductions can unnecessarily get one into trouble. The IRS uses computers to determine who to audit. There are amounts that jump out in the computer's algorithm and raise "red flags" that count towards an audit. A good preparer will have enough experience to know which areas are the trouble zones and steer clients away from that by limiting expenses by playing around with some of the areas that have "wiggle-room" as I like to say, and adjusting depreciation for long term value. We will cover that in later chapters so you understand what to ask for

Now that we've seen the value of getting good help, how do you find a qualified tax advisor? If you needed heart surgery you wouldn't ask your GP to do it. If you wanted a gourmet meal you wouldn't go to Denny's. So how do you know if your neighborhood accountant is up to the task? Education is a start- if they are a CPA or EA they have passed tests and are held to a higher professional standard, also they must take more continuing education every year compared with other designations. But even this doesn't mean anything. Neither does a big business firm pedigree. Just yesterday I did an amended return where the original was prepared by one of the "Big 4" accounting firms- my client is receiving over $10,000 in a refund of amounts they did not need to pay, from the original preparer reporting Puerto Rico income that was not subject to U.S. tax.

So the question remains, how do you find a good preparer? You could ask them questions. Although it often is easier to gauge how good they are by what questions they ask you. If the tax organizer they send you is full of categories of expenses you hadn't thought of before, they ask you questions about the details, such as when you bought property, how much the land value is. Then they are likely doing the research to properly determine your tax situation.

A good preparer also should have time to explain the answers to questions you may have, assuming it is not one of the crunch times just before a deadline and you have an established relationship. A good basic question to ask is for them to explain the difference between cash and accrual accounting. I will get into this in the next chapter, but if they can explain a concept like this in a way you understand it, then they are likely going to be good to work with. Keep in mind though that many accountants these days receive calls from people who are self-preparing returns and want answers to very specific questions so they can do their own on Turbo Tax. So if you get a short answer, don't be too upset. They may be a good accountant, just busy.

Also it is a good idea to ask about the preparer's pricing structure. Often the companies that seem low cost at first glance have very high additional fees for business related forms, especially for self-employment, rental real estate, and employee business expenses. The best preparers will usually have you sign an engagement letter at the beginning of providing services showing an estimate for what you will pay. It is also good to ask if they will be conscious of not charging you fees for services that make less difference to the bottom line than how much the fee is, always a good policy.

> *Tax Tip: It is a good idea to ask up front how much tax preparation will cost. Signing an engagement letter is how many pros let their clients know this.*

With tax being such a complicated area, to get into all the details just is not feasible in a dinosaur-esque encyclopedia set, let alone a single book. So then, what is the purpose of this book? To give you enough knowledge to ask the questions to your advisor that will give you the most tax advantages on your tax return. In the process helping your business be more profitable by being able to make better decisions with an eye to tax planning.

Cutting the Drudgery Out

Saving money on taxes is not glamorous, although it can be fun if approached from the right mindset. Create a special reward for yourself with part of the savings so you have something to look forward to. It is important to remember there is no magic answer that saves you a bundle. Tax savings come in the guise of little tiny changes that seem insignificant when adding them but come together to be big savings. A few dollars here and there may not seem like much, but...

> *Tax Tip: Small savings throughout the return add up to big tax savings in the end.*

Welcome to the world of tax. It's not glamorous, not logical, but not as difficult as many would make it out to be. I like to think of each tax return as a puzzle, with one way it can be put together to make the prettiest picture. Try to keep this in mind while learning about your options and it is a fun process. Saving money should be enjoyable, right?

Chapter 2: Controlling Chaos

Garbage In, Garbage Out.

This old accounting axiom about the initial use of computers holds true. Unless you give your accountant the most accurate information about your tax situation, they are unable to help you save money on taxes, let alone create an accurate return!

It is simple. Whether you are self-preparing or working with a tax preparer, unless you can give them the information that will save you money then you will not receive your fair share of deductions.

Getting Organized

The first step in getting the most advantageous tax treatment is getting organized. Until you know what you are working with you won't know how much savings you need. Ideally you set up a system that allows you to stay organized throughout the year so you can also make accurate projections of what your future tax liabilities will be.

A quick and easy way to take a step in this direction is to form separate bank accounts for business and personal, or even for different aspects of your business. This also helps keep you from commingling funds, which if you ever get audited will help keep your personal finances from coming under scrutiny.

> *Tax Tip: Open a separate bank account for each business venture and be disciplined about using that only for the associated business. Makes accounting for spending much easier.*

Shoebox accounting.

Oh the dreaded shoebox! Every accountant cringes seeing a client carry that into the office. Still, a shoebox worth of receipts is better than no receipts. But it's your job to get them ready and totals written down before going into your tax appointment.

There are some better technology based solutions available now. Scanning and storing receipts on the cloud makes it easy to keep track on a regular basis. Many different types of software, apps and web based services are available that allow you to scan and upload your receipts and tax forms. Some are integrated with your bank account information directly, some even include a live accountant who analyzes and inputs the data into a spreadsheet or accounting software for you. Pretty convenient!

However, the shoebox has it's place. It is still a good way to keep those receipts for the dreaded "just in case". It's a good idea to jot a name of the client, what you discussed at the meeting and the date, on the back of each receipt. This way you can see real quickly which receipt went with which credit card statement and there is no trying to remember who it was with or the business purpose down the line. Also sometimes receipts fade over time so this keeps the important information legible.

> *Tax Tip: Write on the back of each business receipt the client's name, what was discussed at the business meeting, and the date.*

Spreadsheets

The question often then is, how best to organize? From an accountant's perspective, what matters is that the information is understandable and accurate. Quickbooks produces very nice and easily readable reports. The trouble is, it's a full-featured accounting software and so many client's don't know how to use it that they end up with all kinds of mistakes. The most common error I see is that clients will have Quickbooks set to accrual for the accounting type, when they are actually using cash accounting. We will cover this concept fully in chapter 5 where we talk about cost of goods sold.

Chapter 3: Tax Concepts

How much will I owe?

Most of the time the answer is, "less than you think". But this is not always the case and a number of factors come into play. In order to have an idea of what your tax liabilities will be you need to have a basic knowledge of tax concepts.

Also there are many different types of taxes including federal, state and self-employment tax. How and when these taxes come into play is often far more important than the actual tax rates- as you will see clearly in the state tax section.

Tax Rates

Federal tax rates vary from 10% to 39.6%, the highest tax rate coming in for those earning a little over $400,000. But this is only part of the story, how we are taxed is far more complex than this. There are additional taxes such as Social Security and Medicare, collectively known as self-employment tax for those who are business owners adding an additional 15.3% to roughly the first $100,000 of income. We will get into this more specifically in chapter 7 when we discuss employment taxes and employees.

Different types of income are computed different ways. Capital gains tax is the tax for assets such as real estate or ownership of a business that you have owned for longer than one year. Capital gains tax rates range from 0% to 25% depending on the tax bracket you are in. We will discuss this in detail in chapter 9.

Also how the taxable income is figured is nearly as important as the tax rate for determining how much you will actually owe. Several aspects come into play for figuring this, including filing status, the number of dependents you are allowed for exemption amounts, and either the standard deduction or itemized deductions. For higher earning taxpayers AMT can also come into play. First we will cover filing status, exemptions and deductions, then we will get into what actually constitutes taxable income.

Filing Status

The IRS defines five basic types of ways you can file your tax return, the basic categories are as follows:

- Single- you are not currently married and don't have children.
- Married Filing Jointly- a married couple filing a return together.
- Married Filing Separate- each spouse files a separate return.
- Head of Household- if you have dependent children and could file as single or married filing separately you may instead qualify as Head of Household.

- Qualified Widower- if you have lost your spouse in the last few years you may qualify to get tax treatment similar to Married Filing Jointly.

There are several differences of how filing status affects your tax return. For starters, the income levels where the tax rates come into play vary for each type of filing status. Married filing joint has the lowest tax rates for the same income, Head of Household is somewhere between married filing joint and single, and married filing separate will incur the most tax on the same income. This is especially prominent in higher income brackets. For example, if you earn $140,000 per year, you will be in the 28% bracket if you are filing single or head of household, 25% if you are married filing joint, and 33% if you are filing married filing separate. Also the income level where the higher AMT tax rate comes into play is half for married filing separate what it is for all other statuses.

In addition to controlling tax brackets, your filing status affects the level that various credits are allowed in your tax return. Especially with married filing separate status many credit qualification levels are lowered to a point where the credit is essentially disallowed.

Another big way filing status affects your return is the standard deduction amount you are given. Standard deduction amounts for 2014 are $6,200 for single or married filing separate, $9,100 for head of household, and $12,400 for married filing joint.

Standard deduction limitation amounts don't affect everyone as there are two basic ways to compute deductions on the tax return. One option is itemizing deductions on Schedule A and the other is the standard deduction. Itemizing is great for those who have significant home mortgages as they can deduct the interest payments they make in addition to taxes paid and certain business expenses. As this is a book on business taxes we will not go into depth on itemized deductions as it takes a good bit of time to cover this and most accountants handle itemized deductions well. What is important to know is that you can choose to either itemize or use the standard deduction.

In some cases, such as if you have extremely high state tax refund in a year, there is benefit for choosing the standard deduction even if itemizing gives a bigger refund. In this situation, the following year that large state tax refund would be considered taxable income and it could raise the adjusted gross income up to a much higher tax bracket, leading to a large balance due. This often is the case in states that demand large real estate withholding amounts on home sales even though the income will be only partly taxed at year-end.

At other times it may benefit to file itemized deductions even when the standard deduction is higher. This is common in certain states that give very low standard deductions relative to the Federal. Also, at certain income rates itemized deductions become limited, essentially raising the actual highest tax rates slightly over what is listed.

Exemptions

The other basic aspect that affects how much tax you pay is if your exemptions. For 2014 the personal exemption amount is $3,950 and you get an exemption for yourself, one your spouse if you are filing jointly, and then one amount for each dependent. Basically each human body gets an exemption amount, and who can claim this depends on the rules of dependency, i.e. who pays the bills.

Who counts as a dependent? There are two general categories, children and relatives. To be a qualifying child they must be under 19, or 24 and a full time student, they must live with you at least half the year, they cannot have provided over half their own support, and must legally be your child. To be a qualifying relative they must earn less than $3,900, you must provide half their support, and unless they are a close relative such as brother, sister, parent or child, they must have lived with you for the full year. It is good to note that tax exempt income such as certain social security payments do not count as income for this.

Determining Income

Now that you understand how tax is calculated on income, it is important to understand what actually constitutes taxable income. This is real easy to figure out for those who work jobs, as all their income less a few payroll deductions such as contributions to a 401k account are fully taxable. Then there are a few items that can be deducted from that as adjustments to income to determine the magical "adjusted gross income" that the majority of tax rules use to determine eligibility for deductions and credits.

For those who own businesses it is a bit more complicated, but in a good way as those complications equate to tax savings. All the expenses related to their business are taken out before the income is figured, leading to lower adjusted gross income amounts for the same overall gross income. This is why owning a business can be so valuable tax-wise.

Expenses are at the heart of saving money on taxes. First of all, you have to make sure you are in a position to make use of these expenses. When you work a standard job and receive W-2 income you don't get many deductions and the ones you do are reported on Schedule A, after adjusted gross income is calculated, and reduced by an amount equal to 2% of your adjusted gross income before you see the first dollar of tax deduction. Therefore, it is important to own a business. Even if you work for a living, having a part time business in the same field allows you to deduct some of your expenses your would not otherwise be able to deduct.

Unless you have a non-competition agreement in place, it is advisable to go into business in the same area of expertise you already work in. Many people get themselves into trouble by starting businesses that are far from what they know how to run- and end up losing money. Sure, this gives you a tax deduction, but losing money is never a good investment strategy. Yes, it is not so exciting to open a business doing the same work you do all week long. But if you are trying to make a big change, best to either do what you know will make you money and make a lot of it. Then you will have the freedom to do anything you want. The other option is to shift careers through the education and job method, a safer and more profitable way than learning through owning a business, as even taking a pay cut at a new job is smarter than losing money owning your own business, and tax deductions only help in small ways to lessen the sting of losing money.

Owning a business is not for everyone. But for those who do, it can have a number of tax advantages. These advantages can be maximized in some situations by creating entities, we will get into that in the next chapter.

Hobby rules.

One last important element to note is that it is critical that you go into business with the intention of making money. If this is a fun sideline business it is even more crucial that you document carefully that you are intending to make a profit at this venture. Keep records of the amount of hours you put in, how much you spend, and how you are marketing your goods or services to the public.

> *Tax Tip: Keep good records to prove you are running a business for profit. If your business is redetermined a hobby you will lose all your deductions for each year you were in business!*

To avoid classification as a hobby it is wise to not continue a business for many years with large losses. The way it is viewed by the IRS is if, in general, you are running a business for longer than three years and losing money, you are not really trying to turn a profit. I can understand their point. After a few years of losing money on a venture it really is well past time to pivot to some other way of making money.

Forming business entities such as an LLC or corporation also help to show you are serious about your business and not just losing money with your hobby. But even with those entities it is important to either become profitable at a point, or to close the business. Otherwise be sure you are very well documented on the ways you are attempting to make the business profitable.

Chapter 4: Entity Choices

Like First Impressions...

How you form your business is everything. It can have a huge impact on taxes, financing, the complexity of your life, and how professional you come across as being. Not every business needs to be formed as a separate entity, and in some states such as California the hassles and expense of forming an LLC or corp can sink a business before it ever really gets going. So if you live in a state with high franchise fees and corporate tax rates you may wish to wait until your business is turning a profit before incorporating. In other states such as Hawaii and Nevada these fees are minimal and forming and maintaining a business can all be done online in as easy a fashion imaginable. In chapter 12 we will cover state taxes more in detail

Every entity choice has a proper time and usage. Too often I see people with complications more than their situation warrants, or the wrong types of entities for what they need. Thus taking time and money away from what is really important- making a success of their business. This chapter is just an introduction to the subject, covering it thoroughly would fill many books, possibly a whole legal library, and bore you to tears. Before starting any business, it is a good idea to obtain local legal counsel in the locality where you are forming the business.

Sole Proprietorship

This is the most common type of business started by an individual generally from their home without filing any business documents. Tax filings are included in the individual's tax return reported on Schedule C. Liability is unlimited and depending on the type of business may put the taxpayer legally at risk. Hassles of filing paperwork and keeping up the company are minimal, and closing the company often is no more effort than marking a check-box "final year" on the Schedule C.

Filing Schedule C makes it easier to deduct certain expenses such as auto expenses, as the standard mileage rate can be used. And it is easier to use the business use of home worksheets to deduct home expenses as it integrates with the personal return. However many deductions are limited, business use of home for example is limited to the income earned in a certain year.

We discussed hobby rules a bit earlier, but let me stress that when running a sole proprietorship it is important to document that the business is being entered into with the intention of earning money. Otherwise at some point the IRS can disallow any losses you may have as being considered to be partaking in a hobby, not a business. This is an issue that has many court precedents with the taxpayer winning their cases, but clear documentation showing marketing attempts and that the products or services you offer are being offered publically are critical to having this stand up. Also it is not a good idea to have more than a few thousand dollars of losses offsetting your other income. While on occasion this may be sustainable and worthwhile, in general it is asking to be audited.

Qualified Joint Venture

This is an election that can be made to treat a business that is owned and operated by two spouses as a Schedule C business rather than a partnership. Both spouses must make the election and both must participate materially in the running of the business. For each year's tax return filing all income and expenses will be split 50/50 and two Schedule C's will be included in the tax return, each showing half of the income and expenses. This can be beneficial if your spouse helps out in your business as a way to give both spouses social security benefits from the SE tax paid on the income earned without needing to file a partnership return.

> *Tax Tip: A qualified joint venture can be used to split self-employment income with a non-working spouse so that both benefit from the SE tax paid, thereby accruing social security benefits.*

Partnership

When two or more people own a business the default business entity is a partnership. The business partners generally compile the income and expenses each has earned as part of the partnership and the tax return is computed on Form 1065 allocating to each partner their due share, reported to them on Form K-1. Partnerships must apply for an EIN number from the IRS, this can be done online or over the telephone and must be done before the deadline for filing without extensions, in essence- by April 15th of the following year.

Liability defaults to being unlimited, with each partner potentially being responsible for other partner's actions. However, partnerships can be formed as Limited Partnerships (LPs), where one or more partners are designated as general partners and other partners are considered limited partners who do not have control or liability. In this situation, a corporation is often the general partner. This is commonly used for oil and gas pipeline companies that publicly trade small ownership amounts of these partnerships for investors who wish to receive cash payments with paper losses issued on the K-1 for tax reporting time.

There is a big risk with partnerships that there may be tax owed when the interest is sold or the business is closed after taking passive losses for many years. Unlimited amounts of capital can be contributed by partners and this will remedy that situation by raising basis. But losses without additional capital contribution lower basis, potentially leaving the partner with ordinary income when the partnership interest is sold. This often is especially an issue for investors in publicly traded partnerships as all the paper losses over the years of ownership lower basis leading to a large ordinary gain upon sale. This is often a big surprise to investors as their advisors that told them to buy and sell these partnerships did not warn them about this potential tax consequence.

Partnership tax return filing can go from simple to complex, depending on the size of the business, the types of credits and ownership status. How much this will cost to prepare usually depends greatly on this complexity, but it will never be as inexpensive as filing just a personal return. Also the deadlines are more serious- extensions must still be filed by April 15th, but September 15th is the final deadline. The penalties for missing these deadlines are severe- $195 per partner for each month past April 15th, for up to twelve months.

There is, however, a small partnership exception to these penalties that thankfully applies to most taxpayers in this situation. If you have less than 10 owners of the partnership, and all owners are U.S. persons, corporations or estates of deceased partners. All income and expense items must be shared equally, meaning no guaranteed payments. A husband and wife are treated as one partner for this, and a "flow-through" entity such as an S-corp cannot be an owner. If you qualify for this exception attaching a statement explaining this to the return may help, but usually it will have to be requested from the IRS after your tax return has been filed, and you have received the penalty notice.

Limited Liability Companies

While LLCs are not technically a tax entity, they are very common and deserve to be discussed. Tax-wise LLCs are allowed to choose if they wish to be considered a disregarded entity and have the owner file either as a sole proprietorship or a partnership return, or they may elect to be treated as a corporation by filing form 8832. This election to be a corporation can be filed at any time, when filed it is considered as if the partnership has contributed all assets on that day to the corporation and that the members have been issued stock in exchange for their share. If desired, the company can then file to be treated as a subchapter S-corporation. Talk about limitless options!

This flexibility in tax treatment is just one reason that LLCs and LLPs have become popular choices for forming companies in recent years. They offer a good deal of asset protection, especially if assets are broken up into many LLCs, a strategy espoused by many investment gurus. While this can be a good strategy, it also can have complications. Each LLC will have formation and maintenance costs, and if you own property jointly, a partnership return must be filed.

In general, LLCs are used most often for owning real estates and creative companies, LLPs are utilized often in professional fields such as accounting and law firms. Whether one is preferable over the other often depends on the state, Nevada LLCs are the preferred choice and from Delaware I often see LLPs. Be forewarned however- owning real estate in an out of state LLC often means you need to register as a foreign business with the state you own the real estate in. I've seen this commonly as an issue in California- where the $800 minimum franchise tax for LLCs doing business in the state can add up quickly to be a very expensive way to own real estate with no real advantage for properties valued less than a million dollars. Having an umbrella policy and owning the property through a family trust can accomplish most of the goals for many real estate investors without the added complications of managing an LLC.

> *Tax Tip: In some states LLC's come with high annual franchise tax fees and are not worth the additional hassles and complexity. In those states umbrella insurance is a much more reasonable way to go.*

However, if you don't live in a state where this is an issue, an LLC can be a good way to own a business with many options for how the income is treated for tax purposes. Also if you live in a high tax state and are planning to move elsewhere, then owning a company in a state without a state tax can be advantageous down the road as long as your business is not related to earning income in the state of your prior residence. With internet businesses and telecommuting options this is becoming more and more common and can be quite an advantageous plan.

Corporations

The classic entity of choice with a long history of use, dating to Roman law from the 6th century! Corporations are considered more than a separate entity, they are considered a legal person as far as the law is concerned. There are even cases where corporations have been convicted of very human criminal offenses such as fraud and manslaughter.

As corporate law is very well established with regards to limiting liability, it is the strongest choice in that direction. And in the US as state law reigns supreme, Delaware is generally the state of choice for forming corporations because of their long history of clear legal decisions in favor of minimal liability from corporate ownership. This is why many venture capital firms that will require companies they invest in to be incorporated, or reincorporate, in Delaware.

Corporations must file form 1120 or 1120s each year, filing an extension or tax return three months after the end of the tax year, meaning March 15th if using a calendar year. Which form is filed depends on whether the company wants to be considered an "S-corp" or "C-corp". There are advantages to both depending on the situation and we will discuss this a bit, but most small businesses benefit from filing as S-corps. In order to be considered under the Subchapter-S corporation definition that we will collectively call "S-corp" in this book, refers to your company must be owned by US individuals, have less than 100 shareholders and only one class of stock. Additional rules apply, but those are the main ones.

If you are interested in reading more I have included a link at the end of the chapter to the Cornell Law School's website where they have reprinted in full U.S. Code § 1361, the code governing the creation of S-corporations. Also, some corporations such as personal service companies, where most of the income comes from an individual's services, are required to be formed as S-corps unless certain exemptions are met. Generally, this refers to professionals such as doctors, lawyers and accountants.

> Tax Tip: The main benefits of forming an S-corp are that dividends are passed through without being taxed at the corporate level, and are not subject to SE tax. Win-win.

Making the subchapter S election allows the profits of the corporation to be passed through as dividends to shareholders, without double taxation. This means earnings are not taxed at the corporate level, only at the individual level. Also, these profits are considered passive and therefore not subject to self-employment tax. However, it is important to set up payroll and pay a portion of the income as wages for personal services to shareholders if they do work in the business, so that the IRS does not come in at a later date and determine dividends as being self-employment earnings. In addition, S-corps must pay out all profit annually as dividends, otherwise it faces taxation on the leftover retained earnings.

Many of the credits and deductions that are available to C-corps, such as employee fringe benefits, are limited to S-corps. So it is a good idea to research carefully which deductions and credits may benefit your situation best before choosing to file the S-corp election. Also, once you have made the election to become an S-corp you cannot file a new election to become a C-corp until five years have passed unless you lose S-corp status from no longer qualifying to be considered that.

To be treated as a subchapter S corporation, an election must be made on Form 2553. This election must be made within two months and 15 days into the tax year it will be elected in, meaning it is important to file this form immediately after creating your corporation if you wish it to be classified as an S-corp.

> Tax Tip: If you have formed your corporation already and not filed the S-corp election in time there may be relief available to you, contact your tax advisor to see if the exceptions available may apply in your case.

C-corps have more credits and fringe benefits they can be used for, however it is important to carefully structure expense spending documenting business purposes and stay within the legal boundaries. Gone are the days when the C-corp can own everything the employee uses at no cost to an owner/employee. Now that will quickly be redetermined as a taxable employee benefit or a dividend, and taxed accordingly. Many of the transactions between corporations and partnerships start to get into the grey areas of the law. Also, the laws relating to corporations are constantly changing and being redefined, as nearly every bill through congress has secret tax implications. I will address this, and avoiding tax shelters in chapter 15.

Back to practical corporation aspects, one important thing to note is that balance sheets are not required for either partnerships or corporations with gross income under $250,000 and assets under $250,000 for corporations or $1,000,000 for partnerships. Just one of the many reasons why real estate should never be owned in a corporation, rather in an LLC and/or trust structure.

Exit Planning

It's easier to plan the divorce while still in love with the business. Having an exit strategy is always smart, and this should contain how to dissolve the entity. Before forming a corporation look into how complicated it can be to dissolve this entity in the specific state you are forming it in. Often corporations can be quite challenging to get rid of. Another reason why it can be wise to wait on forming one until your business is already profitable and you can really benefit from the structure.

Links:

Cornell Law full text of U.S. Code § 1361
http://www.law.cornell.edu/uscode/text/26/1361

Chapter 5: Accounting Magic

Masters of Fianancial Illusions

Accountants are the masters of illusion in the business world, it always amazes me the clever new ways that big corporations have used to show their income as higher for investment purposes, or lower for tax purposes. In this chapter we will discuss the main accounting concepts that are used to create this magic: accounting and inventory methods.

Accounting Methods

There are three basic accounting methods used by businesses, cash, accrual and hybrid. Cash accounting is what you are already familiar with in your personal life- you report the income you are paid within the calendar year, and you deduct expenditures as they come in. Quite simple and easy to account for.

Cash accounting is most likely what you will use when owning and running a small business, at least at first. This is the type of accounting that will match up to what your bank balances show most closely and minimize confusion come tax time. With Cash Accounting your income is reported when the payment is received, expenses are reported when paid, very straightforward.

Accrual accounting is a bit more complex to learn how to use, but actually shows more accurately what your business has earned. With accrual accounting you report income when the sale is made, i.e. when the contract is signed, and expenses when they are used, rather than when they are paid. Because there is no way to have large payments in one year that are used in other years, this means that some of the spikes of income and expenses are balanced out a bit, giving a more even view of earnings.

As of the printing of this book, there is a tax reform law in the senate requiring all businesses to use accrual accounting, if this passes it will be chaos for many business owners when it goes in. But as of now it has not passed and likely will not.

Under the current law, corporations are required to use accrual accounting unless they fall under the qualified small business rules meaning your gross income was less than one million for each of the last three years and your company is not considered a tax shelter. Also businesses who carry inventory are generally required to use accrual accounting, unless they meet other exceptions, or are granted a different accounting type.

For example, under accrual accounting if you pay a year's worth of insurance on October 1st and your tax year ended December 31st, you would only report ¼ of the amount paid on your current year's tax return. If you paid the same insurance payment on a Cash basis you would deduct the full amount on your current year's return.

Some businesses also use a hybrid method, which is not really a separate accounting system but a combination of accrual and cash accounting. There is no one single system of hybrid accounting, often a combination of cost, gaap and managerial accounting methods is used. As there is no standard system, companies are able to improvise some in how they report income and expenses.

The hybrid method has a number of benefits, mainly in that there are no hard and fast rules for how the accounting is done. Hybrid accounting also gives a good micro and macro view of the company's finances, allowing clear decision making and planning to be done.

Determining a Tax Year

One aspect that influences how you run your business and when you need to prepare your taxes is if you are organized on a calendar year or a fiscal year. A calendar year is the year ending December 31st that most individuals use. A fiscal year can be elected for most business entities if a good reason exists, and can allow that business to end their tax year at the end of any month.

C-corps can easily make this election, but other entity types must show good business reason of why this represents a more natural tax year for them. Examples of businesses where a fiscal year makes sense would be a ski resort, as year end is in the middle of the busy season it is difficult to gauge the profit of the business at that time. Also when it is their busy season it does not make sense to be spending time on accounting and worker's contracts are normally in the middle. Retail businesses also commonly choose a fiscal year as inventory calculations in December are challenging with the holiday busy season.

It is common to end a business in March, June, or September for a fiscal year, as this lines up easily with payroll filings. Most publicly traded corporations try to choose a date to end their fiscal year that will show large last quarter earnings as this seems to excite investors.

Costs of Goods Sold

Costs of goods sold, or COGS for short, is where the costs of the products you sell are reported. These are what people refer to when they say "Above the line costs"- i.e. they give you the directly related costs to the goods or services you are selling.

For self-employed service businesses and professionals you will have very little in the COGS section, so you may wish to take a cursory glance at the rest of this chapter then skip on to the next chapter that will include all the deductions that are much more likely to benefit you. Any type of manufacturing, retail or wholesale sales business will need to break out their expenses related to COGS, so if you have that type of business you should pay attention closely to this chapter.

Now let's get into the details about how the information for Cost of Goods Sold should be presented. To keep everything simple I like to use the order these items are presented on the IRS forms. This way when you give the information to your accountant you will have it presented in an order they are acquainted with, even if they don't use it that way in their own software or ask for it in this order in their tax organizer/questionnaire.

Inventory

You will need to report both the beginning and year-end inventory every year. Be sure the beginning of the year inventory matches the year end inventory from the prior year. Seems like common sense, yet I see that mistake all the time and am always asking clients to explain why the numbers don't match up.

> Tax Tip: Always double check to make sure your beginning of the year inventory matches the year-end inventory the year before, or attach a statement explaining why it has changed.

There are two general methods used to compute inventory- FIFO (First In First Out) and LIFO (Last In First Out). The names are pretty self-explanatory with regards to what they mean, it is an accounting way to manage rising inventory costs, and there can be tax advantages either way depending on your situation. Essentially with LIFO you pay less tax in the current year as the newest items added to inventory are the ones considered sold to offset the purchase. Gives a very current view of the costs of doing business as it shows clearly what you are paying now for each item sold. Whereas FIFO reflects profit more accurately by showing how smart you were to buy before the prices went up.

FIFO businesses will always carry higher inventory costs relative to LIFO businesses. Often LIFO inventories are significantly understated with regards to their value, a good thing to look for when buying stocks as eventually others will get wise to the inventory a publically traded company is holding. But let's get back on the tax subject. S-corps are required to use the FIFO system and if converting from a C-corp to an S-corp there may be a LIFO difference tax to pay the first year of S-corp status.

Purchases

These are all the purchases you made that relate directly to the items you sold. Say you have an eBay business where you buy knick-knacks at garage sales, this is where those items would be listed. You would not list items such as an iPad or Computer here, unless those are the goods you are making or selling.

Personal Use Items

That really cool lunchbox you were going to re-sell but just seemed too cool and you wanted to keep. This is where that item, or anything else you decided to keep, would go.

Cost of Labor

If you have people working for you creating goods, this is where you would list the cost of their labor. Keep in mind, if they are creating goods for you under your guidance they will probably be considered employees with all the payroll needs associated with that such as filing W-2 forms and withholding taxes. We will get into that in the next chapter more in detail.

One important aspect to remember about the cost of labor is that you cannot deduct your own labor- unless you pay yourself wages or issue a 1099 in your name, then you must report that income on your personal return. There is no free lunch in the tax world. In general, your time is considered a capital contribution and is not taxable or deductible, also it does not increase basis.

Materials and Supplies

Many items could fall under this category. If you are building goods this is where you report your raw materials. For an example, if you sew clothing your fabric and thread would go here, but the pre-made hats you buy and also sell on your etsy page would go above in purchases.

Other Costs

This includes additional costs that are essential to sell your product, but not directly part of making or buying it. For example, if you use packaging that is custom printed, it could be listed here under other costs.

How COGS is Useful

After going through this more in detail you should now have a better idea of what goes in the Costs of Goods Sold section, and what types of businesses need to keep track of this. COGS can be very beneficial especially in the early years of running a business where you likely are not making much profit, if any at all. Rather than showing big losses, the goods you have not sold are carried as inventory in lean years. Then in future years when profits are high inventory can be reduced through selling items at a loss or donating to charity. This is why many retail chains compete against themselves with lower priced outlet stores. Moving inventory at a loss can be a terrific tax savings and generates additional income and brand recognition.

> *Tax Tip: In the early years of running a business having a lot of expenses under COGS that increase inventory can help carry expenses to future years when they are needed as more items are sold.*

Common items that shouldn't be listed under COGS but might logically seem like they would include: shipping costs, online listing fees, and sales commissions. A good rule of thumb is if it happens in the process after the item is placed in inventory, it probably does not belong in COGS and would instead be a deduction, In the next chapter we will focus on maximizing deductions, the meat of saving money on taxes.

Chapter 6: Deductions

Deductions

Very few areas in tax law give you the bang for the buck that deductions can have. Yet, there is no one size fits all solution for deductions. Just about anything in the world can be deductible under the right situation, as long as the intention behind running the business is to turn a profit, and that expense has a legitimate business purpose. The general rule for when something is deductible is what the IRS refers to as "ordinary and necessary". If the expense you refer to is ordinary in your line of business, and if it is necessary to your earning income, then it is likely deductible.

I will now alphabetically go through some common deductions that are applicable to many businesses, shining light on some hidden deductions, and mentioning some areas where I see many clients get in trouble. A tax organizer with these categories that you can copy out of the book and fill in is available at the end of this book in the appendix section.

Accounting

Amounts you pay for bookkeeping, business tax preparation and payroll services are deductible the following year. Always check that your tax accountant includes the right amount of tax prep fees, sometimes the tax software doesn't carry this over properly.

Advertising

This refers to traditional and online media costs. Promotional costs and gifts should be listed separately and have different rules for their deductibility. Tax time is a good time to review your marketing plan's effectiveness, comparing with the amounts spent the year before relative to gross income. If you are spending the same in advertising dollars and your income has gone down, it probably means you need to change your advertising angle.

Auto Expenses

The rules for auto expenses are fairly complex, in many books a whole chapter is dedicated to this. But as I'm not giving you full rules but some general guide points I'm just going to go through the basics here. Auto expenses are one of the areas where it is easy to draw an audit with high expenses, so if you live somewhere like LA where driving is a huge amount of everyone's business, be sure to learn these rules very carefully and keep clear records of your business use.

Generally you will get only a percentage of your auto expenses as a deduction, based on how much you actually drive it, or the number of miles used. Want to make all your auto expenses deductible? Here's a simple tip- put a business decal on the side of your car advertising your company.

Instantly all of your auto expenses are deductible because the vehicle is considered 100% business use when you use it as a rolling advertisement. However, this sign must be prominent and permanent, like the signs on construction trucks or those vehicles covered fully with a decal. Magnetic signs and license plate brackets do not count. But the cost of purchasing magnetic signs and custom license plate brackets can still be deducted. Also you have to use a bit of common sense to determine if it really should be considered an advertisement worth full business deduction. In example, a plumbing van covered with decals would be a 100% business use vehicle, whereas a Ferrari advertising a law firm most likely would not be considered 100% business use even if covered in a full wrap decal, unless it is parked in a prominent location, such as on the side of a highway advertising vehicle crash lawsuits.

> Tax Tip: Using your vehicle as an advertising platform may allow 100% of auto expenses to be deducted, but it must serve genuine business purpose to hold up in tax court.

If you plan to fully deduct auto expenses, be sure the vehicle is owned in the name of the business entity, otherwise it may be disallowed. Also in this case it may fall under the fringe benefits rules. As this is a complex issue I would highly recommend getting a professional to review your auto deductions to make sure you are meeting the most current tax court rulings related to this. There was a tax court case in 2010 where it was disallowed to deduct auto expenses based on advertising on license plate brackets. I have included the link at the end of the chapter, it is an interesting read to get an idea of the intention behind the auto laws as determined by the tax court and what is and is not acceptable.

Mileage vs Actual Expenses

Deducting mileage is simpler and often more valuable unless you drive very few miles, lease a vehicle, have a very expensive vehicle, a vehicle that uses a lot of gas, or a large truck. Also partnerships and corporations cannot use the standard mileage rate, however they can reimburse employees for auto expenses using the standard mileage rate. The amount deducted is added to the employee's W-2, then the employee can deduct the standard mileage again on Schedule A under business expenses, but this amount is reduced by 2% of adjusted gross income before being used as a deduction. The standard mileage rate has gone down from 56.5¢ per mile in 2013 to 56¢ per mile in 2014. So if you drive the average 12,000 miles a year and pay more than $560 per month in the vehicle expenses listed below, you may indeed benefit from using actual expenses.

The year you place the vehicle in service you must choose to use the standard mileage rate if you wish to use it in future years. Then in the future you may switch back and forth between standard or actual expenses. This can be a wise decision if you tend to keep vehicles for a long time, or don't need a large depreciation deduction in the year the vehicle is placed in service. Sometimes actual expenses will qualify you for a very large deduction in the year the vehicle is placed in service, in chapter 8 I will go into the various methods of depreciation in the year you buy a vehicle.

Whether you use the Actual or Standard Mileage deduction method it is important to note that parking and tolls are always deductible as an additional amount, and the receipts as such should be kept separate.

> *Tax Tip: Amounts spent for parking and tolls are deductible in addition to actual or standard mileage expenses, so be sure to compute them separately*

Vehicle expenses include:

Insurance

Auto insurance is obviously deductible. If it is packaged with other insurances such as home insurance for a discount be sure to allocate a portion of the discount percentage to reduce the insurance deduction.

Registration

The Vehicle License Fee portion of your registration is considered a tax that can be deducted on the Schedule A itemized deductions or allocated between business and personal. The rest of the registration fees are considered a business expense, but if you only use a your vehicle partially for business it is worth breaking the licensing fee portion out separately so the personal portion can be deducted as well.

Repairs and Maintenance

Big repairs are usually obvious, but the little costs such as oil changes or a tire repair are often forgotten. It is a good idea to go through the car's glove box at tax time to make sure all vehicle expenses have been accounted for.

Lease Payments

Figuring out the deduction for lease payments is a bit complex as the IRS has an inclusion amount that must be deducted from the lease payments to figure the amount that is deductible, that makes this amount more comparable to the depreciation on a new car that was purchased. This is a good thing to approximate and figure out when comparing the advantages of leasing or buying. For more information on lease payments please see IRS Publication 463, link provided at the end of this chapter.

Interest Payments

The interest you pay on the purchase of a vehicle is deductible. Your principal payments are not. The principal portion of the vehicle is part of the basis that is used in depreciation, explained in chapter 8.

Parking and Tolls

The parking meters that accept credit cards are one of the greatest inventions ever- instant proof of the meter amounts paid! Other options for keeping track of parking meters is to keep a log book in your car or on your smartphone or tablet and jog down the amounts when used. Do keep in mind that Parking and Tolls are still deductible in addition to using the Standard Mileage deduction method.

Washing

Washing your vehicle, whether at home or at the car wash is deductible as part of auto expenses. Keep track of those amounts.

Signage

Permanent and removable signs, custom license plate brackets, and full vehicle wraps are fully deductible as a business expense.

Tickets

Parking and traffic tickets are never deductible. Makes paying for parking garages seem that much smarter.

Bank charges

Monthly bank charges are deductible, so are fees for services such as wire transfers, online bill pay services, and check printing. Overdraft fees and other fines are not deductible.

Business Use of Home

While there are many telecommuting fantasies of lounging poolside in slippers, or relaxing on the sofa typing away on your laptop, it's tricky to get the IRS to agree that either of those visions would be considered a home office. In order for office space to be tax deductible it must fall under one of the following sets of rules:

1. A principal business space used only for business purposes, and used regularly.
2. A space you use exclusively and regularly for meeting with clients.
3. A separate structure from your main house used for business purposes.
4. Your total home is used as part of a daycare facility.
5. Storage space for business items.

To determine the part of your home office usually a percentage of the office square footage divided by the home square footage is used. It is helpful sometimes to draw the floorplan out to determine this and keep it in your business documents for reference. Deductible expenses include the business portion of rent, interest, real estate taxes, insurance, utilities, maintenance, repairs and depreciation. It is good to not that lawn care is not deductible, nor is painting or remodeling any room in the house other than the home office.

The tax court has recently determined that those who live in small spaces such as studio apartments may have their offices in the same living space- but the caveat is that it must be legitimately an office where you meet with clients, have office furniture such as desk and shelving, it must be your main place of business, and for your employer's convenience. Still, this is a huge recent win for small business owners who operate out of small apartments, just because you don't have a separate room for your office does not mean it is not allowed as a deduction any longer.

Having a home office has a big advantage many don't think about- if your primary office is in your home you have no commute. Therefore, all the miles you drive for business count as business miles. If you have a separate office and drive to locations directly from your home otherwise the miles would not be counted as business miles.

> Tax Tip: If you have a home office as your primary business location, all miles driven for business are deductible.

Home office expenses for self-employed and employees generally must be reported on form 8829. For partnerships and corporations the portions of business related home expenses (as figured by percentage of use generally) must be reimbursed to the partner/employee, and then the portions paid by the company can be deducted on the 1065 or 1120. In certain circumstances it may make sense to own your home in an LLC that rents the business space to your corporation or partnership. This can be a good way to simplify the deduction, but be careful as there are closely held company rules to ensure this is not a way to get around paying a dividend. Be sure to document the fair market valuation carefully so as not to have it considered an excessive payment.

There also is a relatively new safe harbor rule that gives your $5 per square foot of office space to deduct each year up to 300 square feet. With this rule you don't need to prorate any expenses and your mortgage interest and property taxes are still fully deductible on Schedule A. The biggest advantage of the safe harbor method is that as it does not include depreciation when you sell your home you will be covered by the homeowner's exemption and not fall under the depreciation recapture rules at that time. A big bonus for homeowners who don't want to recapture depreciation under the allowed or allowable rules down the road (please see chapter 8 for more details about this).

Cell Phone

Cell phone deductions get into one of those grey areas. If you use it more than 50% for business you may be able to deduct a percentage of your usage, or the cost of additional features you use specifically for business. For example if data tethering is something you use and the cost for iPhone data without tethering is $20 a month, but the cost with tethering is $50 per month, then the $30 difference is deductible.

Beware of flat-rate services- in a 2005 tax court case the court determined that on a flat-rate service none of the cost was deductible (Ritchie, TC Summary Opinion 2005-181). The following is from this case- "Petitioner's cell phone was a personal phone that he also used for business calls. Petitioner testified that he paid a flat rate, regardless of phone usage. Therefore, aside from the personal expense of the phone, which is rendered nondeductible under section 262, he incurred no additional charge for business use."

I would still say this is one of those grey areas that may be redetermined at a different time and for many businesses there are cell phone deductions that can be taken. As long as you keep records showing the percentage of business use, a portion of the bill may be deductible, depending of course of your line of business and how needed your phone is.

For employees, cell phones can be considered a legitimate business expense if they are required to be reached at all time, such as management or sales representatives. If this is not the case, then they are considered a fringe benefit, we will cover fringe benefits and their tax consequences later.

Commissions & Fees

If you pay commissions and fees to a corporation, or certain other business entities, then you do not need to issue 1099 forms. However, if you pay over $600 in one year to an individual, you must file a 1099-misc form reporting their income. This will be covered in more detail in chapter 7.

Computer

Computer repairs and software purchases are deductible. Computer and other large equipment purchases must be depreciated, see chapter 8 for more information about depreciation.

Delivery/Freight

Delivery costs are deductible both on goods you sold and purchased.

Dues/Subscriptions

Any publications that are industry related you subscribe to are deductible, as are professional memberships. However, memberships in "lifestyle" oriented organizations such as country clubs are not deductible.

Educational

Continuing education related to your business is deductible. If the education is for learning something unrelated, such as pursuing a new career, it is not deductible. But these educational costs may qualify for a credit. Remember you cannot use the same expenses both for a deduction and a credit, you must choose what is most beneficial.

Employee Benefits

Fringe Benefits will be covered in chapter 7 when we discuss employment.

Entertainment

This is where the tax code gets fun. Taking a group of business associates out to a nightclub and buying bottle service is a tax deduction, as long as all members of your party are business associates not social connections (i.e. no wives- having them around would lose a portion of the tax deduction). And people say Congress doesn't watch out for it's own interests in the tax code. All joking aside, you can deduct the full expenses including the portion for your spouse and/or a client's spouse if you can show a clear business purpose for the meeting.

Also, in general, you can only deduct 50% of the amounts paid for entertainment costs. This is a fun area to save a lot of money in, I'd highly recommend reading through Publication 463 and learning the ins and outs of what you can deduct for there are probably a number of situations you didn't realize were business events that you could deduct. The link to Pub 463 is in the end of the chapter.

Gifts

This is one of the more commonly misunderstood categories of deductions. There are two main categories of gifts. The first is subject to a $25 per person limit for gifts you give. This limit does not count extras like engraving or packaging and shipping costs. Say I need to send a gift basket to thank two business associates at one office, this means I have a $50 budget to keep it within, plus shipping costs.

Certain gifts could also be considered Entertainment or Promotional, this is one of those areas where you can have a little wiggle room and depending on your situation and what you need deductions-wise, get more or less out of how much you spent.

Insurance

Most common types of insurance such as liability, property, E&O, worker's compensation and umbrella policies are deductible.

Medical insurance if you are self-employed or have a partnership or S-corp must be reported on the front page of the 1040. This means it is an adjustment to income, lowering federal tax but not offsetting self-employment tax. For partnerships and S-corps the insurance plan can be in your name or the business's but if it is in the individual's names the business must reimburse you for it and show the payment to you on Schedule K-1 in order to take the deduction.

C-corps still have full deductions for medical insurance and employees are not subject to social security and medicare withholding on those amounts. However they do have some restrictions related to coverage provided to key employees-meaning executives and employees who are at least 5% owners.

Janitorial

Janitorial or house cleaning costs are deductible. If it is for a home office they will be prorated for the space used as an office and may part of Business Use of Home.

Laundry & Cleaning

If you are on a work trip and you need to have clothes cleaned, or if you have uniforms that are required for your work, the laundry or dry cleaning costs are deductible. Regular dry cleaning of suits and such are not deductible.

Legal & Professional Costs

Legal and professional costs are deductible only if they relate to earning income. When you are starting a new company and pay these costs prior to launch they are amortizable. In chapter 8 amortization will also be covered.

Licenses & Permits

Most licenses and permits associated with your business are deductions. Costs related to obtaining an immigration visa are not deductible to employees, the employer portion of certain fees are however. The costs of maintaining commercial driver's licenses are deductible. The costs of getting or renewing a standard vehicle or motorcycle driver's license, are not.

Meals

Meals are subject to the 50% rule, unless you meet the transportation exemption such as truck drivers, and have a number of rules to qualify under similar to entertainment, the main item to remember that if it is really splurging, relative to the restaurant of course, they may not be a deduction. For more information see publication 463 listed at the end of this chapter.

For travel there are per diem rates that can be used in lieu of actual expenses when travelling for most business purposes. These amounts have been frozen from increasing for 2014. The current rate for most US small localities is $46 per day. For more information on per diem rates you can view the GSA website, link at the end of the chapter, they are who determine the per diem rates the government and most businesses conform to.

Office/shop Expense

If you have a separate office space you rent/own it is fully deductible, calculated similar to business use of home. If you keep a storage area for storing business equipment or a safety deposit box for business documents that is also deductible.

Outside Services

In general, this would be where you would list any labor that you issue a 1099 for if you pay an individual over $600 in a year. Also if you have temp services you pay through a service they would go here. Be sure to follow the rules about who is an employee. For more information on this see Chapter 7.

Pest Control

If you need pest control for an office or rental property it is fully deductible. If it is for a home you keep an office in, then this falls under the business use of home rules.

Postage

Both postage machines and individual stamps are deductible. Nearly every business should have some amount listed here, if only a small amount as it is rare not to have some mailing costs during the year. But so often I see no amount listed here, pure laziness on the part of the preparers to ask about this. A few dollars may not seem like much, but every little bit adds up to big tax savings.

Printing

Brochures, catalogues and flyers go here. Beyond the basics it is good to keep in mind when printing small promotional items such as pens or mugs there is a $4 per item limit, not including personalization costs, as discussed under the gift rules.

Professional Viewing

This is a commonly forgotten item for those in the entertainment industry. If your business involves making TV shows or movies then the cost of cable TV and movie tickets are considered a deduction. One of the great examples of how anything can be deductible if it is ordinary and necessary for being successful in your business.

> *Tax Tip: If you are an actor/writer/musician or involved in other creative business you may have professional viewing deductions for cable TV and movie tickets.*

Promotional

Events and giveaways can drive big business your way. Be cautious of the limits listed under gifts and entertainment. Also keep in mind that these types of things can get out of hand real easily. Don't end up like the dot com businesses of the 90's, many who sank themselves on promotional expenditures that never added up to earning a dime.

Refuse Disposal

Another expense to remember to include in business use of home if applicable or separately listed for independent offices. Shredding services are also deductible.

Rent- Office

Office rent is fully deductible, as long as it is not paid to a related company, in that case it is deductible if not excessive. If you own your building under a LLC and are renting yourself an office out of it for more than Fair Market Value you are potentially getting yourself into trouble. This is a legitimate business strategy however, just be sure to document the value of your office by searching comparative prices and documenting this before settling on a price.

Rent- Equipment

Equipment rental is generally deductible. The exception being when there is only a nominal payment at the end to purchase the equipment, then it may be redetermined to be a purchase agreement and considered interest and principal. The key in this is to structure the purchase price at the end of the lease being at least significantly larger than a single rental payment.

Repairs

Repairs of business equipment are deductible. Just be sure to keep track. Repairs are surprisingly easy to forget about come tax time. Wanting to forget about the struggle surrounding hassles like a dead computer battery is very human.

Retirement Plans

Please see chapter 17 for details about deductible retirement plans.

Salaries and wages

Please see chapter 7 for details on payroll deductions.

Samples

Deductible, but be sure to keep track of which customers samples are provided to. Items withdrawn for personal use are not deductible.

Security Service

Prorated as part of business use of home if associated with residence, otherwise fully deductible.

Small Equipment

Equipment and tools that are inexpensive and/or could be considered to have a short lifespan. If you buy equipment that has a life expectancy of five years or longer it should be depreciated.

Start-up Costs

When you have just formed your Corporation or LLC, any cost incurred before the date of formation fall under start-up costs and must be amortized. Generally this includes things such as corporate formation documents, legal services and registering the company's domain name.

Storage

Maintaining a storage unit for business supplies is deductible. Also, a portion of your home used exclusively for business storage can also be added to the percentage for business use of home.

Supplies

When purchasing business supplies at places like Costco or Wal Mart, it is a good idea to separate them out from personal items at the register and make two purchase transactions. This way it is clear come year end how much was spent without prorating sales taxes.

Taxes

Local business taxes and employer payroll taxes are deductible. Property taxes are deductible to the extent of business use of home, if applicable, the the personal amount can be deducted on Schedule A if itemizing deduction. Foreign taxes are more complicated and will be covered under the foreign section.

Telephone

A separate land line used solely for business or a VOIP line is deductible, as are business Skype calls.

Travel

The IRS defines this as traveling away from your general business area for longer than the course of a single day, but less than a year. Travel includes temporary work assignments, however if you are gone for an indefinite period of time it no longer counts as travel and you are considered to be living in the new location.
Travel expenses include airfare and other transit costs, lodging, meals, tips, dry-cleaning and shipping goods. But if the cost of something is free, such as using frequent flier miles, there is no deduction.

> *Tax Tip: Save free comps, such as using frequent flier miles and loyalty points for personal trips and pay for the business related travel so it can be a deduction.*

Instead of deducting actual expenses, per diem rates for high and low cost localities are posted that can be used. The rules for travel deductions are frequently changing. Before making any travel plans that you expect to be deductions I would recommend giving publication 463 a thorough read.

Foreign travel has some additional restrictions. To be fully deductible foreign travel must meet one of the following sets of rules:

- the trip must be fully for business,
- you had no control over making the business arrangements,
- the trip was for less than one week,
- less than 25% of your time was spent on personal activities, or
- a vacation was not a major consideration.

It is doubtful if the IRS would question a business trip to Iraq as being for a vacation, unless you have family there. A good detail to note here is that if you work on Friday and work on Monday the weekend in between is counted as business days because you were on standby waiting for your next business meeting. Therefore any sightseeing or visiting friends over the weekend does not make the trip any less of a deductible business trip.

Utilities

Water, gas and electric costs are deductible for your separate office or prorated as part of business use of home. Internet costs may be fully deductible if used just for business purposes depending on the line of business and how web oriented it is.

Virtual Office/Assistant

As this is becoming more common I have included it here. Do remember that if you hire an individual in the U.S. as a remote assistant you must file a 1099 for them if you pay them more than $600 within a year.

Web Services,

IT, web design and other Internet related business services are deductible.

Links

For more information on the rules and details of the deductions you can take in your business I would suggest reading:

IRS Publication 463, Travel, Entertainment, Gift and Car Expenses http://www.irs.gov/publications/p463/index.html

Tax Court Case:
http://www.ustaxcourt.gov/InOpHistoric/WILLOCKC.TCM.WPD.pdf

GSA Per Diem Rates:
http://www.gsa.gov/portal/category/104711

Home Office Tax Court Case: Summary Opinion 2014-74,
http://ustaxcourt.gov/InOpHistoric/MillerSummary.Guy.SUM.WPD.pdf

Chapter 7: Employees

Who Is An Employee?

Somebody has to do the work in every business. When it is time to expand and hire on help then you will need a little bit of knowledge to avoid a whole lot of trouble. How that worker gets paid has several possibilities, keep reading to learn the advantages and disadvantages of various ways of handling the issue of employment.

First it is important to discuss who is considered an employee. If you hire someone to work in your home or business, you supply the tools they use to work on and direct how they do their work, then they are an employee. If you have someone come to work for you, but they run a business that they market to the public offering similar services, they are probably considered an independent contractor. This line can be a bit vague at times. The general rule is how much control you have over what the worker does. It is common for professionals such as doctors, lawyers and veterinarians to be considered independent contractors.

It is important to define this properly, through clear contracts with workers and using the appropriate terms. Independent contractors should never be referred to as employees in communication of any sort. Also, be forewarned, that no matter how much you document it, if you are trying to disguise employees as independent contractors and they really are working as employees, eventually you will get caught. The IRS allows for employees to file a statement with their tax return stating that they were not an independent contractor but rather an employee, and they are allowed to only pay half of their Self-Employment tax with the return when filing, meaning you will get a bill in the mail for the other half!

> *Tax Tip: Be sure that your workers are aware that as 1099 workers they do not have payroll taxes withheld and they will owe at the end of the year.*

Your workers may say all is well and good and they are fine with being 1099 workers, before they get the tax bill at the end of the year for 15.3% of their earnings. Owing many thousands of dollars in tax can change minds very quickly. But working as an independent contractor allows them to deduct their expenses against their income as well, meaning they pay far less taxes than they would otherwise, so it is in their benefit in the long run. However rational this is though, the emotional pain of owing tax can often displace both logic and common sense. I've seen it hurt business owners too many times.

Independent Contractors

If you have someone working for you and they fall under the independent contractor rules, then you will need to file form 1099 on their behalf if you paid them over $600 in a year. Form 1099 must be filed by February 28th if you do paper forms or March 31st if you e-file the docs. If you file more than 250 forms 1099 you are required to electronically file. The form must be provided to the worker by January 31st. As independent contractors are expected to file their own tax return where they pay Self-Employment tax, you are not required to withhold any taxes on their wages.

Employees

When your workers fall under the employee category, your life gets a bit more complicated. You must withhold FICA taxes for Social Security and Medicare, federal and state tax withholding amounts, and federal and state unemployment tax. Plus if you offer group medical or 401k plans you will have more withholding requirements based on that. We will cover each of the classes of withholding below.

When these payroll payments are due becomes a bit complicated. Please see the chart in appendix for a quick breakdown of when many payroll taxes are due. In general payments must be made through the government's free electronic payment site, more information about this and all these topics can be found in the IRS' Publication 15, link at the end of the chapter.

Statutory Employees

There are a handful of jobs that meet the federal requirements for not being employees, but the employer is still required to withhold Social Security and Medicare taxes, and sometimes pay unemployment taxes. This usually is just for delivery drivers, homeworkers who follow specific guidelines and certain salespeople. If one of these applies to your business I would recommend doing more research and getting a professional opinion before determining if you can have your workers perform their duties as independent contractors.

Forms Employees Must Fill Out

You must have employees fill out forms W-4 for their tax withholding, and form I-9 to prove they are legal to hire. New hires must be reported to the state you live in so if they have child support or other payments garnished from their wages you will know to take that amount out.

FICA Taxes

Most taxpayer's don't realize they are paying over 15% of their wages out as Social Security and Medicare taxes! I've always seen this tax on the employer's side as something of a secret tax on Americans, and it just keeps increasing. The FICA tax income withholding limits continue to rise, Social Security Tax being now 6.2% of wages up to $117,000, and the employer must also withhold from the employee's paycheck an additional 6.2% contribution up to the same limit. Medicare demands an additional 1.45% tax from both the employer and employee, and the employer is expected to act as third party for this amount also. In addition to that, Obamacare added a 0.9% additional medicare tax to all wages over $200,000. Children under 18 working in a business owned by one or both of their parents are not subject to Social Security and Medicare taxes.

Federal and State Withholding

To determine federal withholding amounts, you will have the employee fill out form W-4. IRS publication 15 has tax tables that based on the W-4 information you can determine how much to withhold. If your state has an individual tax then there will be additional instructions for withholding, contact your local franchise tax board to find out the instructions if you are unsure of when you need to file and with which forms. Please see chapter 12 for more information on state taxes.

Unemployment Taxes

Federal unemployment, or FUTA, is 6% of the first $7,000 paid to an employee. If you pay into a state unemployment also, then up to 5.4% of the state unemployment tax can be used as a credit against the federal FUTA, leaving just 0.6% to be paid in to the feds. If you hire a parent, child or spouse you are not required to pay FUTA taxes on their behalf.

If your state also has an unemployment tax you will need to contribute to their withholding cutoff as well.

Tip Income

If your employees earn tip income you must ask them to give you this information for you to withhold taxes on. You are required file form 8027 reporting this by February 28th of the next year. A credit in the amount of FICA taxes you pay on their tips is available as part of the general business credit.

Fringe Benefits

The rules for fringe benefits have become stricter and stricter as Congress's way of trying to stop wealthy taxpayers from giving themselves tax free advantages such as flashy vehicles. Generally the rules for deducting vehicle expenses are much more relaxed for self-employed taxpayers and employees, so these days it is better to own vehicles in your own name rather than the business name, unless your business is heavily car related such as a dealership or construction company that would need to own many vehicles that would fit within the constraints of the fringe benefits rules. For the most up to date information on Fringe Benefits you can see the IRS's Pub 15B, the link is at the end of chapter. Following is a chart of how various fringe benefits are treated, please keep in mind that most of these lose some of their tax exempt status if the plan favors key employees (i.e. executives or more than 5% owners), and many of the deductions are limited for S-corps.

Fringe Benefit Tax Treatment

Type of Fringe Benefit	Income Tax Withholding	FICA Taxes	Federal Unemployment
Health Insurance	Exempt, except for S-corp owners and long-term care benefits.	Exempt, except for S-corp employees who are 2% shareholders.	Exempt
Achievement Awards (goods, not cash)	Exempt up to $1,600 for qualified plan awards ($400 for nonqualified).	Exempt up to $1,600 for qualified plan awards ($400 for nonqualified).	Exempt up to $1,600 for qualified plan awards ($400 for nonqualified).

Adoption Assistance	Exempt	Taxable	Taxable
Athletic Facilities	Exempt if substantially all use is by employees and their immediate families, and the facility is operated by the employer on premises owned or leased by the employer.	Exempt if substantially all use is by employees and their immediate families, and the facility is operated by the employer on premises owned or leased by the employer.	Exempt if substantially all use is by employees and their immediate families, and the facility is operated by the employer on premises owned or leased by the employer.
De Minimis Benefits	Exempt	Exempt	Exempt
Dependent Care Assistance	Exempt up to certain limits, $5,000 ($2,500 for married employee filing separate return).	Exempt up to certain limits, $5,000 ($2,500 for married employee filing separate return).	Exempt up to certain limits, $5,000 ($2,500 for married employee filing separate return).
Educational Assistance	Exempt up to $5,250 of	Exempt, up to $5,250 of	Exempt, up to $5,250 of

	benefits each year.	benefits each year.	benefits each year.
Employee Discounts	Exempt up to certain limits.	Exempt up to certain limits.	Exempt up to certain limits.
Employer-Provided Cell Phones	Exempt if provided primarily for business purposes.	Exempt if provided primarily for business purposes.	Exempt if provided primarily for business purposes.
Group-Term Life Insurance Coverage	Exempt	Exempt up to cost of $50,000 of coverage.	Exempt
Health Savings Accounts (HSAs)	Exempt for qualified individuals up to the HSA contribution limits.	Exempt for qualified individuals up to the HSA contribution limits.	Exempt for qualified individuals up to the HSA contribution limits.
Lodging on Business Premises	Exempt if furnished for your convenience as a condition of employment.	Exempt if furnished for your convenience as a condition of employment.	Exempt if furnished for your convenience as a condition of employment.

Meals	Exempt if furnished on your business premises for your convenience.	Exempt if furnished on your business premises for your convenience.	Exempt if furnished on your business premises for your convenience.
Moving Expense Reimbursem ents	Exempt if expenses would be deductible if the employee had paid them.	Exempt if expenses would be deductible if the employee had paid them.	Exempt if expenses would be deductible if the employee had paid them.
No-additional -cost Services	Exempt	Exempt	Exempt
Retirement Planning Services	Exempt	Exempt	Exempt
Transportatio n (commuting) Benefits	Exempt up to certain limits if for rides in a commuter highway vehicle and/or transit passes	Exempt up to certain limits if for rides in a commuter highway vehicle and/or transit passes	Exempt up to certain limits if for rides in a commuter highway vehicle and/or transit passes ($130), parking ($250),

	($130), parking ($250), or qualified bicycle commuting reimbursement ($20).	($130), parking ($250), or qualified bicycle commuting reimbursement ($20).	or qualified bicycle commuting reimbursement ($20).
Tuition Reduction	Exempt if for undergrad education (or graduate education if the employee performs teaching or research activities).	Exempt if for undergrad education (or graduate education if the employee performs teaching or research activities).	Exempt if for undergrad education (or graduate education if the employee performs teaching or research activities).
Working Condition Benefits	Exempt	Exempt	Exempt

Links:

Payroll forms including 1099 forms that must be filed can be ordered from the IRS' website:

http://www.irs.gov/Businesses/Online-Ordering-for-Informati
on-Returns-and-Employer-Returns
IRS Publication 15 (Employer Tax Guide):
http://www.irs.gov/pub/irs-pdf/p15.pdf
IRS Publication 15b (Fringe Benefits):
http://www.irs.gov/publications/p15b/ar02.html

Chapter 8: Depreciation

Depreciation Basics

In my first tax course the teacher introduced depreciation as, "this is the topic to pay attention to if you want to make a lot of money as a tax preparer. Depreciation is what separates the good preparers from everyone else." She was right, depreciation is one of the most important methods of personalizing a tax return to be most advantageous for a company's overall situation. It shocks me how often I review other preparer's returns, and see a total lack of depreciation, often to a huge disadvantage to the taxpayer.

What is depreciation exactly? Nothing in life lasts forever. Everything is considered to have a useful life period. This is the allotted time the government says that a structure or item's value is reduced to nothing and then must be remodeled, or rebuilt. For example, 5 years is considered the lifespan of a car, 7 years for office furniture, 27.5 years for a rental house, and 39 years for a commercial building. There may be some truth to that. I drove by a house in the Kahala neighborhood of Hawaii the other day that looked to have been built in the 1980's and the roof was caving in from age and lack of maintenance. I guess thirty years really is the approximate lifespan of a house in the tropics! In most parts of the country houses last longer than this, but the depreciation amounts must be a "one size fits all" solution. There are two choices for the way depreciation can be taken- accelerated or straight-line. Most tax software defaults to accelerated depreciation. This depreciates property over the shortest time and gives the biggest deductions in the first couple years, then less deductions later. There also is an alternative depreciation method available, that can often be beneficial. This uses as straight-line method to depreciate the property over a longer period of time, by an equal amount each year. All real estate is depreciated using the straight-line method, although a longer alternative time frame of 40 years is available. Typically I will ask business clients if they think they will make more or less money over the next couple years and tailor their depreciation choices to meet their business needs.

> *Tax Tip: If a business is not yet profitable, or if a taxpayer is limited in the amount of deduction that can be taken, alternative depreciation is a smart bet as it saves more deduction for future years when larger deductions are needed.*

Beyond choices related to lifespan, depreciation is calculated slightly different for houses and goods. How this affects you, is how it is deducted, based to when the item is placed in service. Houses are always depreciated on a mid-month convention, meaning they are considered to be placed in service in the middle of the month purchased in.

Depreciation on houses is always straight-line, and the same for each year. Goods are either considered placed into service in the middle of the year, or if many goods were purchased near the end of the year then the depreciation for the current year must be considered placed in service on a quarterly basis.

On the quarterly system, goods are depreciated starting in the quarter they were purchased in. This law is meant to limit companies from making a huge amount of capital purchases in the last month of their tax year after forecasting how much tax they will pay. One of many ways in which forecasting and tax planning year-round pay off, as this allows business purchase decisions to be made throughout the year. Also good to note this as the car companies often have big sales near the end of the year, but your tax deductions may be limited if you buy the car at that time. Always something worth weighing into the costs of purchasing any large capital item.

Section 179 Expensing

Small businesses have a special depreciation deduction available to help them known as Section 179. This law allows businesses who purchased less than $2 million worth of capital goods within the tax year, to expense goods they bought in the year they purchased them, rather than depreciating them over many years. Section 179 deduction is available for most new and used good placed in service, including certain software. The American Taxpayer Relief Act that was passed to avoid the "fiscal cliff" in 2012 raised the amounts of 179 deduction to $500,000. However, this amount has not been renewed for 2014 yet and is slated to return to $25,000 that was the allowed amount over a decade ago.

Generally though, this is the type of deduction that will be extended last-minute.

One business strategy of Section 179 deductions has to do with leases on vehicles or business equipment. Since the IRS determined lease payments that have a nominal cost (often $1) to purchase the property at the end of the lease to actually be sales, this means that you can lease property and take a full section 179 deduction in the year of purchase- often generating a tax savings larger than the first year's payments. Of course, this means future payments are not deductible, unless an interest portion has been determined. So this must be planned well with regards to future cash flow.

Bonus Depreciation

Congress loves to pass special depreciation laws that allow greater amounts to be deducted. This bonus depreciation gives a deduction of 50% of the purchase price of new property placed in service, encouraging new purchases. Bonus depreciation is only for brand new property, and cannot be used for software purchases.

This tax break has been around in one form or another for the last decade, but is slated to expire after tax year 2013. The House of Representatives approved a bill to make this law permanent starting in 2014, but it has stalled in the Senate as they like to wait until after midterm elections to pass tax laws.

Again, this is something that normally defaults when placing items into tax software for depreciation but is often not the best treatment of assets for small business depreciation purposes. Nice to have this option available sometimes, but in most cases I use Section 179, accelerated and straight-line depreciation methods in order to better allocate assets into the depreciation classes that give the client the greatest balance of short- and long- term benefits. After November though, it will be clear which combinations of depreciation will be of most benefit in the next couple years.

Listed Property

Certain items such as cars and computers have historically been purchased and placed in service in ways that have violated the spirit of the depreciation rules leading to them being classified as listed property. By definition, listed property is property that can be easily used personally by employees. This includes: computers, entertainment equipment such as camera equipment, vehicles with gross weight of less than 6,000 lbs, and other transportation property such as motorcycles and boats.

In order for listed property to be deducted at all, they must be used at least 50% for business purposes. Any personal usage is considered non-deductible, and all expenses must be allocated accordingly. If listed property does not meet the primary use test of 50% then it also is not property that Section 179 or bonus depreciation deductions can be taken on.

Recapture When Sold

The rules for when you sell a property deduct "depreciation allowed or allowable" meaning even if you don't deduct depreciation, you still have to pay tax when you sell the property on the depreciation you could have taken! Depreciation recapture will be covered in chapter 9 when we discuss sales.

Amortization

Similar to depreciating an expense over the straight-line method. Certain expenses, such as business start-up costs and research and development costs, are eligible to be amortized and deducted over a number of following years. You can choose the amortization period for a corporation or partnership, any period up to 15 years is generally approved. Although once you choose a period you are stuck with that.

Amortization is beneficial in that it allow you to spread costs in a high spending year to future years when the deductions may be needed more. Especially for startup costs, and similar section 197 intangibles, which include patents and branding costs, this is very beneficial, as usually in the first year of a business profit is nominal.

Chapter 9: Sold!

Capital Gains Tax

So you've sold a property, piece of equipment, or your whole business, the big question looms: How much is Uncle Sam going to hit me for?

If you've held the property for less than a year it is considered a short term capital gain, if you hold it longer than one year it is a long term capital gain. Even with the recent increases, long term capital gains are a relative bargain compared to the rest of the tax code- 0, 15, or 20% tax rate depending on your tax bracket.

If your total income including the capital gains, is under $36,900, or $73,800 for married couples, this means you have a 0% tax rate on the capital gains. But be careful- if your adjusted gross income goes over those amounts you will owe 15% on your capital gains plus being pushed into a higher tax bracket for your income taxes.

Capital losses if short term are fully deductible against earned income, if passive are only deductible to a maximum $3,000 per year against ordinary income and otherwise just available to offset future capital gains.

Net Passive Investment Tax

However it is not this simple anymore- now you will fall under the "Obama Care" rules net passive investment tax if your gross income is over $200,000 ($250,000 for married filing joint status, and $125,000 for married filing separate). This equates to a 3.8% additional tax to fund the US insurance companies, whoohoo! I'm not a huge fan of "Obama Care," aka the "Affordable Care Act," if you haven't figured that out yet. I'm all for public health insurance and think it works great how it is set up in Europe or Canada. Just, in the U.S., it was done in the most wasteful and expensive way they could do it by forcing taxpayers to purchase plans through the avaricious insurance companies. Rather than being a safety net it has turned into a spider's web of tax complications that many people will find themselves caught in for years to come.

But I digress, the new net passive income tax is here to stay. This brings the effective top capital gains tax rate to 23.8%. My big issue with this tax is the way it is implemented. It comes in at the bottom of the second page of the 1040, meaning this tax comes in after other credits are taken against income. So, for example, if you have foreign tax credits on your interest income that would normally wipe out your tax, and would wipe this tax out as well, as they come in before the net passive income tax on the 1040 they cannot be used to offset this tax and you will still end up owing regardless of foreign taxes paid.

If you earn over $200,000 a year leaving your money in the bank earning .03% interest is now even more poor of an investment than ever before. Another reason tax-exempt bonds are of more value than ever before. Or for those who sell stocks and are in higher income brackets the "growth hurdle" of additional gains the new stock. For someone who plans to hold the new stock for 10 years this equates to needing an additional gain of 1.38% annually over the stock sold in order to break even.

Qualified Dividends

But even with these higher tax rates dividends are often still a good investment choice tax-wise. As qualified dividends are taxed at long-term capital gains rates. To be considered qualified the stock owned must be a U.S. or foreign company traded on U.S. stock exchanges, and the stock must have been held for 60 days of the 121 days prior to the ex-dividend date, meaning the day after declaration of a dividend where the purchaser would no longer be entitled to that dividend.

Recapture of Depreciation

Regardless of income exclusion and long term capital gains tax rates, if you have depreciated the property you sell, or the sale of your business includes depreciated property, then you may be subject to recapture of depreciation upon sale. How much tax you pay on this depends on what class the income falls under. But, in general, if you took depreciation on business property and sold the property any gain over the depreciated basis is taxable at a 25% depreciation recapture rate.

It is important to note that this is based on depreciation allowed or allowable, meaning even if you did not take the deduction you may be subject to depreciation recapture same as if you did, and the maximum amount. This is why it is so important to really think about depreciation when preparing a tax return, if a sale is coming up with in the next couple years selecting a longer depreciation schedule may prove very smart. There are some exceptions to depreciation recapture for investors in low income housing developments, with up to 50% of the recapture excluded.

Collectibles and Personal Property

Personal property such as a car, when sold should be reported if there is a gain, and this falls under the capital gains categories, but losses are not deductible and should be zeroed out. Collectibles are taxed at a collectible capital gains rate of 28%. For those who fall into the range of the net investment income tax of 3.8%, the new collectible tax rate is 32.8%. Items that are considered collectibles include: coins, stamps, art, antiques, classic cars, fine wines and precious metals such as gold and silver. Even mutual funds and exchange traded funds that hold gold for their owners are considered collectibles, and may be subject to a surprising capital gains hit when sold at a profit.

Homeowner's Exclusion

If you have sold a home you have lived in for two out of the last five years you have one of the best tax deals available to you- the homeowner's exclusion. This will let you exclude up to $250,000 in capital gains ($500,000 if married) from paying any tax on. This was huge when the real estate bubble was going crazy, I had dozens of clients every year who took this exclusion and came away with millions tax-free. The last handful of years I have seen less of this. But the real estate market is coming back now, and many who bought at the bottom are cashing in on their home profits.

In certain situations there are reduced exclusions available if you have lived somewhere for less than two years and are forced to move for extraneous circumstances, such as disability, your home being destroyed or condemned, or for active military members. There is no longer a partial exclusion for civilians who have been forced to move for employment purposes.

1031 Exchanges

One potentially good option for deferring gains is to use what is known as a section 1031 exchange to roll the investment in one business property that is sold into a new business property. Using this set of rules the IRS considers it as if you traded your property directly for a bigger one, and considers that reinvestment qualified for tax-deferral. The property traded for must be similar, such as investment real estate for other investment real estate, or one business for another business.

I've been advising clients away from 1031 exchanges for a number of years because of the historically low capital gains rates, except in circumstances where the gains pushed their other income into the highest tax brackets, and they already had investment opportunities in mind, or if they had depreciated the property significantly would face large ordinary income. In many circumstances it made sense to pay 15% tax at the time rather than an uncertain amount in the future. However, with the new net investment income tax and the higher top rate of capital gains, it now makes sense to use 1031 exchanges again.

In order to use a 1031 exchange you must plan this before you enter into a contract to sell your house, as this must be part of the sales contract. You will hire a qualified intermediary that the funds from the sale will be transferred to. This cannot be any company you have any control over or it will invalidate the exchange.

You will have to identify your replacement property within 45 days and complete the transfer within 180 days of your original sale closing. These deadlines run concurrent with one another, so if you identify your property on day 45, you only have 135 days left to close. This timeline can be quite tight for trying to buy replacement property- especially with how long it can take to close on short sale and foreclosure properties lately! You are able to identify multiple replacement properties, generally three is considered maximum. Although you may choose as many as you like, as long as the aggregate fair market value of the replacement properties do not exceed 200%.

> *Tax Tip: Start looking for replacement properties or businesses before yours is sold. This way you can identify your choices right after the sale have more time left to obtain financing and close the deal.*

The replacement property must be "like-kind" meaning if you have a rental house the money must go into other real estate investment property, not commercial property. So you can't sell a rental house and roll the money into a warehouse for your business to use. However, you could roll that money into a commercial building to rent or even raw land. Also the replacement property must be more expensive than the sold property, and the loan must be higher than any existing loan.

This means you must take out a new loan or contribute additional capital to make up the difference. If there is any cash received at the end, or debt is reduced, the difference is considered "boot" and is taxed at normal capital gains rates as an allocated portion of the property sold. The mortgage aspect of this is important to watch. If the property you sold had a $400,000 mortgage on it, and the replacement property has only a $300,000 mortgage, then the $100,000 difference is considered taxable even if the overall purchase price was higher.

1031 exchanges can no longer be done on residences. Sometimes those who have vacation homes will rent them for a period before exchanging to have a tax-free exchange to another property. In general, for this to be valid the property must be a rental for at least six months prior to exchange. This means actually having tenants stay there, not just holding the property out for rental. Then the property traded for has limits on personal use for the first two years of the greater of 14 days or 10% of the total days it was rented at fair market value.

Qualified Small Business Sales

If you sell a small business you may be able to exclude a certain amount of the income if it falls under certain rules, or rollover the gains into another business. Many businesses are disqualified from this. Actually, so many businesses are excluded it is hard to imagine many this applies to. In order to be considered a "Qualified Small Business" your business cannot be any of the following:

- One involving services performed in the fields of health, law, engineering, architecture, accounting, actuarial science, performing arts, consulting, athletics, financial services, or brokerage services;
- Any business of operating a hotel, motel, restaurant, or similar business.
- One whose principal asset is the reputation or skill of one or more employees;

- Any banking, insurance, financing, leasing, investing, or similar business;
- Any farming business (including the business of raising or harvesting trees);
- Any business involving products for which percentage depletion can be claimed;

By the off chance you are lucky enough to own a business that somehow is not any of the above, say an e-commerce website, then you just may have hit the tax jackpot and be able to exclude between 50- and 100% of your taxable income. This law definitely has been a boon to angel investors and often dictates the types of ideas they are willing to invest in so it is worth thinking about these categories for entrepreneurs building a business and looking for venture funding.

Chapter 10: Money, Money

Borrowing Money

There is a story about Donald Trump that always stands out in my mind where his son pointed out to him a homeless man on the street with a sign that said only one dollar to my name. His son told the Donald that he should give the homeless man a dollar, but instead Donald told his son that homeless man was a billion dollars richer than he was, as he was so far in debt.

While earning money through sales is heavily taxed, borrowing money has no tax consequence at all- unless you default on the loan. However, the interest, if used for a business or investment purpose, is deductible. Pretty sweet deal.

Capital contributions also carry no tax burden, therefore venture capital funding also is a deal. And using capital carries no risk of income from cancellation of debt, as we will soon cover. Capital contributions are pooled in the company in exchange for the company issuing new stock with a value in the percentage exchanged. As long as the contributor holds the property for at least a year then the gains they receive when selling their shares are taxed at capital gains rates.

Cancellation of Debt

The Mortgage Debt Relief Act expired December 31, 2013. Therefore taxpayers who sold their home in a short sale or were subject to foreclosure in 2014 may receive taxable cancellation of debt. It will remain to be seen if this will be signed in again last minute to be extended.

As there is no guidance yet issued for 2014 I think it is worth noting the exceptions and exclusions available for 2013 as many of these will likely be extended in November when Congress passes the new tax laws. Canceled debts that meet the requirements for any of the following exceptions or exclusions are not taxable:

Debt Cancellations or Reductions that Qualify for EXCEPTION to Inclusion in Gross Income:
1. Amounts specifically excluded from income by law such as gifts, bequests, devises or inheritances
2. Cancellation of certain qualified student loans
3. Canceled debt, that if it were paid by a cash basis taxpayer, would be deductible
4. A qualified purchase price reduction given by a seller
5. Any Pay-for-Performance Success Payments that reduce the principal balance of your home mortgage under the Home Affordable Modification Program

Canceled Debt that Qualifies for EXCLUSION from Gross Income:
1. Debt canceled in a Chapter 11 bankruptcy case
2. Debt canceled during insolvency
3. Cancellation of qualified farm indebtedness

4. Cancellation of qualified real property business indebtedness
5. Cancellation of qualified principal residence indebtedness

The exclusion for "qualified principal residence indebtedness" provides tax relief on canceled debt for many homeowners involved in the mortgage foreclosure crisis currently affecting much of the United States. The exclusion allows taxpayers to exclude up to $2,000,000 ($1,000,000 if married filing separately) of canceled "qualified principal residence indebtedness."

If you exclude canceled debt from income under one of the exclusions listed above, you must reduce other tax attributes such as credits, losses, basis of assets, by the amount excluded. You must file Form 982 to report the amount qualifying for exclusion. For cancellation of qualified principal residence indebtedness that you exclude from income, you must only reduce your basis in your principal residence.

Currency Trading

In general, holding currency for personal or business purposes then trading for another, for example Euros to Dollars, is not taxable, and there is no filing or reporting necessary. If you are doing currency trading as an investment strategy, such as Forex trading, then there is tax due. This tax is computed using the "60/40" method applied to futures; 60% is treated as a long-term capital gain and 40% is treated as a short-term capital gain. For example, if you are in the 35% tax bracket you would have a 23% blended gain, plus the net investment income tax of 3.8%, or a total tax rate of 26.8% on currency transactions.

Bitcoin Transactions

With the recent popularity of the electronic currency Bitcoin, the IRS has recently come out with their rules defining the taxability. The rulings disappoint many who trade in this currency as they are treated like a stock, subject to short and long term capital gains, rather than as with currency trading in general, where there is no tax event that takes place. Trading in Bitcoins though is treated more like owning stocks or real estate, where the gain or loss is considered an investment. In the future I imagine this will be challenged and may be redetermined, but how it is now, nearly all transactions in Bitcoin are subject to capital gains tax.

The decision that Bitcoin is considered property not currency, is because it is not issued by any legal jurisdiction. Therefore, Bitcoin currency trades must be included in income, reported at the conversion rate on the day received. Short- or long-term capital gain tax then is due on Bitcoin when sold, or used as a payment. Theres is some flexibility with this as the conversion rate average can be figured as you like, but must be applied consistently.

> *Tax Tip: If you have lost money trading or holding Bitcoin, the losses are deductible against other income. Losses in other currency trades are not.*

As some employers have started paying salaries in Bitcoins, this becomes increasingly complex. The pay you receive in Bitcoin is taxed as income at the rate of exchange on the date the payment was received. Then if you keep the funds in bitcoin and later use them to buy goods or services, any gain or loss on the Bitcoin for the conversion rate on the date you used them is considered a capital gain subject to tax, or a deductible loss. Talk about creating a complicated tax reporting situation, as in this case every purchase you make needs to be reported.

Income from mining of Bitcoins is considered self-employment in most circumstances, and both ordinary income tax and self-employment tax is due on the gains received. Also receiving payment in Bitcoin for personal services also may constitute self-employment, and do remember the the IRS taxes all worldwide income. Payments made in Bitcoin to an individual for services are subject to the 1099 reporting rules. And soon businesses will start receiving 1099-k forms for payments received in Bitcoin.

Yes, these rules must be applied retroactively, and the IRS can audit up to seven years in the past. There is amnesty available right now to not pay penalties such as the late filing and underreporting income penalties that can add up to 50% of the tax liability due easily. If you mined or traded bitcoins and have not paid taxes on these transactions I would recommend filing amended returns to correct this.

Chapter 11: Tax Credits

Want Some Free Money?

Tax Credits are the fodder of big corporations. These organizations make many business decisions to take advantage of tax credits, ranging from the location of opening an office, to the type of new business to transition into. Tax credits are interesting to look at, as they are a window into the American political system. Each bill that goes through congress include all types of credits to benefit the politicians' benefactors. Predictably, oil and gas production businesses have the most amount of credits available, many of which I've declined to mention here as I can't picture them benefiting many small businesses. Credits are as changing as the political system, and many valuable credits have not been renewed over the last couple years.

In general, tax credits are more valuable than deductions, especially to taxpayers in lower tax brackets. This is because credits are valued dollar for dollar against tax owed, whereas deductions reduce taxable income at the same tax rate as the individual. So if you are in a 35% tax bracket $1000 worth of deduction will reduce tax $350. In the 15% tax bracket, this same deduction would lower your tax only $150. In this case, a 25% tax credit would benefit the taxpayer in the 15% bracket, but not the taxpayer in the 35% bracket.

> Tax Tip: There is no double-dipping, you must choose whether to take a credit or deduction for each specific expense as most benefits your business.

Credits also have additional value to C-corps in that they may be carried back five years and forward up to twenty. This means that when it is possible to take credits in a year of high deductions, you can choose a previous year where you were more highly taxed and apply the credits there to receive a refund rather than ending up with a negative retained earnings on your books that does you very little good, and looks questionable to investors.

Most credits are only useful to offset tax, but a few credits are known as "refundable", meaning even if you don't owe tax you can get the credit as a refund. Free money from the government. You can't complain about that if you get lucky enough to be one of the ones who qualifies. In this chapter we will cover a handful of individual credits and then go on to the many business oriented credits.

Earned Income Tax Credit (Schedule EIC)

Dubiously known as the "Tax Welfare" system, earned income credit is only available to very low earning taxpayers. Still, this is one of the biggest refundable credits- up to $6,044 for taxpayers with three or more qualifying children. And even very low income taxpayers without children can qualify for a small amount of credit. This makes the earned income credit a huge boon at tax time for many Americans, and fodder for firms that give refund loans to those who want their free government money faster. My first tax job was at H&R block and it was common to have clients that received $8,000 refunds without having paid a penny of tax in throughout the year.

Many others are benefitted by this law however. With deductions from self-employment, many independent contractors who have one or more children find themselves getting a small refund rather than owing big money in self-employment tax. The rules for claiming earned income credit are complex, and for preparers the documentation is high, making many professionals not want to file these returns any longer. Also the audit rate for self-employed individuals claiming earned income credit is very high- as when you are self-employed it is easy to adjust some of the more "variable" deductions to maximize refund. Keep in mind with earned income credit that if you get audited and they find you have more expenses than you reported you will be penalized same as if you had overreported expenses.

To qualify for earned income credit you cannot have more than $3,300 in investment income. For 2013 earned Income and adjusted gross income (AGI) must each be less than:

- $46,227 ($51,567 married filing jointly) with three or more qualifying children
- $43,038 ($48,378 married filing jointly) with two qualifying children
- $37,870 ($43,210 married filing jointly) with one qualifying child
- $14,340 ($19,680 married filing jointly) with no qualifying children

Child Tax Credit (Schedule 8812)

Another child-related credit, but the rules with this one are a bit more generous than the earned income credit with regards to who it applies to. If you have dependent children, you may be eligible for up to $1,000 as a credit for each child. The phase-out for getting this credit begins at $110,000 for married taxpayers filing a joint return, $55,000 if a separate return, or $75,000 for single or head of household status filers. Qualifying children are age 16 or younger at the end of the tax year, and meet the relationship, residency, citizenship, support and dependent tests as outlined in the unified child definition viewable in the credit instructions or in Publication 17.

This is a refundable credit to those who don't have tax liability. Also it has no US residence restrictions making it one of the few credits available to US taxpayers who live outside the country.

Retirement Savings Credit (Form 8880)

If you contributed to a retirement plan such as an IRA or 401k you may be entitled to up to 50% of your contribution as a non-refundable credit of up to a maximum of $1,000, or $2,000 if married filing jointly. This credit phases out at fairly low income levels, fully phasing out at the top end for married taxpayers filing jointly at $59,000.

> *Tax Tip: This can be very valuable if you fall into the right income range as between this credit and the adjustment to income, a traditional IRA contribution can equate to a 65% return on investment just with tax savings!*

For retirement savings contributions it is important to note that contributions to IRA accounts can be made up until April 15th of the following tax year. Therefore early filers should always look to see if this might be a beneficial strategy.

American Opportunity Credit

This gives up to $2500 of credit for the first 4 years of college. Up to $1,000 of the credit is available as a refundable credit. This gives a dollar of credit for each dollar spent on tuition, fees, and course materials- including books and supplies not directly bought from the university. Does not include expenses paid for room and board, transportation, optional student fees, medical fees or insurance. If cost of a computer is required for a course or enrollment in the institution then that cost would be included.

This credit is available for those with incomes up to $90,000 for single, married filing separate and head of household, or $180,000 if married filing joint. To qualify, the student must be enrolled in a degree program taking at least half of the normal full time load of classes and cannot have been convicted of a felony drug offense. That last part always cracks me up- I guess Congress assumes drug addicts somehow should have completed their education before they got strung out. Such a peculiar restriction, but nobody ever said tax law was logical.

As of the printing of this book the House of Representatives have just passed a revision of the American Opportunity Credit that is supposed to simplify the tax code and roll all of the education credits into one, but basically entails just repealing the lifetime learning credit and not renewing the tuition and fees deduction. This bill also cut the adjusted gross income amounts where you could claim this deduction nearly in half. So watch this bill closely if these higher educational credits apply to you, or will soon.

Lifetime Learning Credit (Form 8863)

For those who cannot qualify for the American Opportunity Credit because it only applies to the first 4 years of education, there is the Lifetime Learning Credit to fall back on. Credit is worth 20% of the first $10,000 of expenses, meaning a $2,000 maximum credit. Phases out between $52,000 and $62,000 for single people, and double that for taxpayers filing jointly with their spouse. This credit is slated to possibly be removed for future years.

Foreign Tax Credit (Form 1116)

The foreign tax credit is one of those credits that often sounds better on paper than it plays out. Intended to prevent double taxation, it does not always pan out that way. Although it is based on the full amount of tax paid, the deductions you use prorate out a portion of the credit, and it is reduced by various other factors that often disallow another part of the allowable credit. In addition, separate forms 1116 must be filed for each category of income with income and tax divided between the different income classes. The 1116 is the first credit that gets applied on the credit list, making many credits that would come after it useless.

Even in high-tax countries, because of how the 1116 comes into play on the tax return and is applied, there often is a tax due when filing with only the 1116 to reduce tax liability. And for most investors who have foreign taxes paid on their investment accounts, the actual credit they would be entitled to is so low it is barely worth filing the forms. Also this credit does nothing to offset the Net Investment Income Tax.

Small Business Health Care Credit

A credit of up to 50% of the premiums paid by small businesses to cover health plans for their employees. To qualify for this credit your insurance must cover only employees, not family or dependents, you must have 25 or less full-time employees, and pay less than $50,000 average wages to your employees. The credit is sliding scale, and the lower the average wages you pay, the higher percentage of credit you get. With less than 10 employees and an average wage of $25,000 or less the full 50% credit is available.

General Business Credit (Form 3800)

If you file a tax return as a C-corp, many credits all flow through as part of the general business credit. Generally, the other forms listed here are not filed with a C-corp's return, and the amounts from them are simply included on Form 3800. No credits that flow through onto the general business credit are refundable. However, general business credits may be carried back five years or forward up to 20 years as needed. General business credits also may not necessarily be eligible to offset all tax, how much is eligible is calculated on the credit form.

Investment Credit (Form 3468)

Giving credit for expenditures as varied as adding solar panels, buying an electric vehicle, renovating a pre-1936 building or making coal power plant repairs. Credit varies from 10-30% depending on what the expenditure was for and if it was in an area that was a recent disaster area.

Credit for Employer Social Security and Medicare Paid on Tips (Form 8846)

This credit is to encourage owners of restaurants and bars to get their employees to report tip income and pay FICA taxes on that income. As long as you pay over the federal minimum wage you are able to claim the full amount paid as a credit and it can be carried forward or back as needed. Worthwhile to do for food establishment owners, as it prevents IRS coming in at some future time to audit all employees and determine tips that are taxable.

Low Income Housing Credit (Form 8586)

Real estate developers who wish to set aside 15-40% of their project for low income rentals can get huge refundable credits. To qualify for this credit, you must be pre-qualified for and only so many per state and area are allotted, so if you are not involved in making your project qualify for this since the pre-planning stages it is hard to receive this credit.

American Samoa Economic Development Credit (Form 5735)

Ever wanted to move your business somewhere beautiful, and get a huge tax credit for doing so? If you have certain types of businesses, ranging from architecture to computer software development, there are some huge credits for conducting business in American Samoa. Credits available include 60% of qualified wages paid and 15-65% of the depreciation deductions of business property.

Disabled Access Credit (Form 8826)

This credit allows qualified small businesses to take a credit of up to 50% of the cost of installing equipment and other services that make your business accessible to those who are physically or mentally disabled. There are a lot of options with this credit and it can have many applications, such as adding readers or taped texts for the visually impaired. Definitely a credit worth reading if you are rehabbing a commercial property, or want to expand your business to be able to better serve those with disabilities.

Credit for Small Business Pension Plan Startup Costs (Form 8881)

This credit is for partnerships and corporations with less than 100 employees that form a pension plan. A credit is available for 50% of the costs involved in establishing or administering the plan and educating employees about the plan. Must have at least one employee eligible to participate, who is not a highly compensated employee, to qualify. Note that there is no requirement they do participate, just a requirement they are eligible.

Credit for Employer Provided Childcare Facilities and Services (Form 8882)

This gives a credit of up to 25% of the expenditures of providing childcare facilities and services up to $150,000 in any year. The only caveats being the childcare facilities cannot be on the same property as any employee's residence, and the offering of services cannot favor highly compensated employees.

Distilled Spirits Credit (Form 8906)

Wholesalers of alcohol can benefit from this credit, albeit one must have massive amounts of alcohol warehoused to benefit more than a de minimis amount.

Mine Rescue Team Training Credit (Form 8923)

This credit gives mine owners up to a 20% credit, on up to $50,000, of the cost of training employees for being part of a mine rescue team.

Research Credits

If you are in the scientific field or developing new products you may benefit from research tax credits, although not as many are available now as at times in the past. The credit for Increasing Research Activities (Form 6765) is very narrow credit for those developing new products who have hired others or university researchers to do research or testing on their ideas. The Orphan Drug Credit (Form 8820) is aimed specifically at medical researchers.

Community Development Credits

If you want to form businesses or develop/redevelop real estate in areas that are designated community development zones, you can get some valuable tax credits for doing so. This includes the New Markets Credit and the Credit for Contributions to Selected Community Development Corporations. To do this, you will need to work closely with the community development organizations. It has been my experience these organizations generally will offer other governmental help with issues such as permits, and sometimes even offer to pay for architectural or other business planning services.

Electric and Alternative Vehicle Credits

Several alternative vehicle credits are available. The Qualified Electric Vehicle Credit (Form 8834) and Qualified Plug-In Electric Vehicle Credit (Form 8936), range from $2500-$7500 in credit depending on the type of electric vehicle purchased and how many the manufacturer has already sold. The Alternative Motor Vehicle Credit (Form 8910), covers Honda or Mercedes fuel cell powered vehicles; qualifying for a credit ranging from $8,000-12,000 depending on the model. Surely the car dealership will tell you all about how much credit you may get from buying a particular vehicle. Some credits are limited by AMT, so if that is an issue for you it may be wise to figure the actual credit you can take before purchasing.

Renewable Energy Credits

There are several renewable energy credits that apply to residential and commercial applications. The residential credit is calculated using form 5695. The business credit is calculated with form 8835. The credit amounts vary depending on the power generated. If you are planning on installing solar, wind, geothermal or other renewable energy sources, own multiple properties and a business entity, it is worth comparing the value of the individual and business credits to see which is most valuable in your particular circumstance.

Alternative Fuel Credits

There are a number of credits available to producers of alternative fuels and bio-diesel, as well as to establishing pumping facilities for these fuels. These laws keep getting snuck in on every bill through congress. There was an alternative fuel production credit even as part of the "Obama Care" package- how that has anything to do with health care beats me. If this applies to your line of business then please research the most current laws and credits pertaining to this and keep eyes on developments as they seem to be constantly changing this area.

Chapter 12: State Taxes

Tax, tax and more tax....

State taxes are another issue that is important to plan about. Forming your company in the wrong state can have dire long term consequences, but also people get silly about forming sometimes in different states when it is unnecessary to do so. As it would take an encyclopedia set to fully cover state taxes, this chapter will be a quick introduction to individual and business taxes in all states. Useful for planning initial business moves into other states and including some tips and traps I've run across in the field.

One thing to note is state standard deductions are often low. Sometimes although itemizing deductions on the federal return is not beneficial, on the state tax return it will be. Also please keep in mind that state laws change frequently, for the most updated information always verify before making business decisions based on state tax rules.

Alabama

Alabama personal income tax ranges from 2% to 5%. Personal exemptions are $1500 each, standard deductions range from $2,000-$7500 depending on filing status and adjusted gross income. Social security and many other qualified pensions are exempt from tax. There is no estate tax. Although the official state sales tax is only 4% in some localities it can be as high as 12%.

Alabama has a corporate tax of 6.5% of net income that is due in addition to the business privilege tax that all business entities must pay which is based on net worth varying from $0.25 to $1.75 per every $1,000 . There is a minimum tax of $100 and a maximum tax of $15,000 for most companies. Family owned LLC's are capped at $500. Alabama tax information can be found at: http://revenue.alabama.gov/index.cfm

Alaska

There is no personal income tax or inheritance tax in Alaska. There also is no state sales tax, but some localities charge a tax of up to 7.5%

There is a corporate income tax in Alaska ranging from 1% to 9.4%. The top income tax bracket comes in at a very low $90,000, possibly making this a state where corporations are not the wisest entity structure unless really needed, or structured as an S-corp. LLC's and partnerships must file a biannual business report that costs $100 every two years to submit. Alaska tax information can be found at: http://www.revenue.state.ak.us/ The business portal is at:http://commerce.alaska.gov/dnn/cbpl/Home.aspx

Arizona

Personal income taxes range from 2.59% to 4.54%, the highest rates starting around $150,000. Exemptions are given at $2,100 per person and standard deduction is $4,833 for single taxpayers and $9665 for those who are married filing a joint return. Social security is exempt, pensions are mostly fully taxable, the only exception being military and in-state pensions that have the first $2500 of income treated as exempt. Arizona has no estate or gift tax.

Arizona has a corporate tax of 6.968%, with a $50 minimum tax. Most cities in Arizona also assess an annual privilege tax. Sales taxes in Arizona are complex. The state charges 6.7% and all counties charge an additional percentage, plus many localities, with sales taxes in some locations as high as 13.7%. Arizona tax information can be found at: http://www.azdor.gov/Home.aspx

Arkansas

Individual tax rates range from 1% to 7%, with the highest bracket coming in at a measly $34,000! There is a standard deduction of $2,000 single/$4,000 married filing joint. Rather than an exemption there is a credit amount of $23 per person. Did I really get these numbers right or is somebody at the Arkansas tax board getting real life values mixed up with the prices on the Monopoly board? Wow the cost of living must be cheap there!

Social security is exempt, as is the first $6,000 of pension payments- including IRA distributions. There are no estate taxes. Sales taxes are 6.5%, but food is taxed at 2%, and localities can add up to 5.5% additional to either base amount.

There is a corporate franchise tax that is figured based on stock issued of .3% of the outstanding capital stock or $150 minimum, $300 flat-rate for companies with no capital stock value. $150 flat rate franchise tax for LLC's. Corporate tax rates range from 1% of the first $3,000 to 6.5% of any amount over $100,000. Arkansas does not conform to the federal depreciation rules regarding bonus depreciation, so care must be taken when deciding depreciation methods with Arkansas

income. Tax and business information can be found at:
http://www.state.ar.us/dfa

California

Tax rates in the Golden State range from 1% to 13.3% in the top bracket... hope they give a lot of gold back for demanding that! California has a standard deduction of $3,841 single and $7,682 married filing joint and they also have small personal exemptions and individual credits that apply. Social security benefits are exempt but all pensions are fully taxed. California also adds a 2.5% penalty tax on early distributions from pension funds. California has a refundable Child and Dependent Care Credit. There is no separate estate tax, just a minimal amount that piggy-backs off the federal.

One of the most avaricious states, California makes it rather difficult to move abroad. They consider those who move out of the state still residents unless they have fully severed ties, and will hunt former residents down around the world to send tax bills.

California has sky-high corporate tax rates, with an $800 minimum tax for all business entities doing business in the state. C-corps pay an 8.84% tax rate, S-corps pay a 1.5% tax rate, although financial corporations of either type pay even higher. LLC's are taxed at the corporate rate of 8.84% with the $800 minimum tax. Sales tax is a minimum of 7.5% and can be up to 3.5% higher in localities.

Also it is important to note that some California cities have steep city tax rates based on gross receipts, often due even if the company reports a net loss. City of LA has an income tax that varies based on the type of business, ranging from $1.01 $5.07 per $1,000 of gross income. San Francisco has flat taxes that range from $75 to $30,000, also based on total gross receipts. Additional tax information can be found

at: https://www.ftb.ca.gov/index.shtml   The California
business portal is at: http://www.sos.ca.gov/business/

Colorado

Tax rates here are rather straightforward- 4.63% of
federal adjusted taxable income. Uses federal exemption and
standard deduction. The first $20,000 of combined social
security and pensions are deducted for those between 55-64
years old, or $24,000 for those over 65 years of age. There is
no estate tax in Colorado.

Corporations in Colorado pay a flat tax of 4.63% of net
income, just like the personal taxes. Partnerships and S-corps
do not pay a separate tax but are required to withhold and
pay in the 4.63% tax from partners or shareholders payments.
State sales taxes are only 2.9% but in various localities they
can range up to 9.6%. A periodic report accompanied by a $10
fee is due each year. Colorado business and tax information
can be found at: http://www.colorado.gov/

Connecticut

Income tax rates range from 3% to 6.5%, with a personal
exemption ranging from $12,000 to $24,000, depending on
filing status. There is no deduction or credit amount, and
there is no benefit for dependents. Social Security is exempt
for taxpayers with adjusted gross income under $50,000, or
$60,000 if married. Half of military pensions are exempt, but
all other out-of-state pensions are fully taxable. Connecticut
has an estate tax starting at $2 million in assets at 7.2% and
ranging up to 12% of total assets, making this a pretty
expensive state to die in.

The Corporate tax rate is a 7.5% flat tax. Pass-through
entities such as partnerships and S-corps are required to
withhold tax on payments to partners, or shareholders, if

their share of Connecticut source income is $1,000 or more. Sales tax is 6.35%. There is a $250 annual business entity tax that must be paid by all S-corps, LLCs and limited partnerships. Connecticut tax information can be found at: http://www.ct.gov/drs/site/default.asp Business registration is at: http://www.ct.gov/sots/site/default.asp

Delaware

Personal income tax rates range from 2.2% to 6.75%. There is a $3250 standard deduction and double that if married. There is an individual credit of $110 per person including dependents. Those over age 60 get a double credit. Social security and a portion of military pensions are exempt. Delaware has no sales tax.

One of the more popular states for forming corporate entities, contrary to popular belief Delaware is not a tax-free state. Delaware charges an 8.7% flat rate tax on earnings attributed to the state. So why then are so many corporations headquartered there? Among other things, clearly written corporate business laws especially with regards to mergers and acquisitions attract businesses. Delaware does not tax their businesses on income that is earned in other states.

Delaware has a franchise tax that those who form companies there need to watch out for. If you do not assign a par value to your stock, or assign too high of par value, you can end up with sky-high franchise tax rates. Hearing of clients that got a $30,000 bill in the mail for their first franchise tax payment on a startup is not uncommon. Best to obtain legal counsel when forming in Delaware as it is a legally complex state, which is why it is so beloved by corporate lawyers. Delaware tax and business information can be found at: http://revenue.delaware.gov/

District of Columbia

Personal tax rates range from 4% to 8.95% with a personal exemption of $1675 per person and a standard deduction of $2,000, doubled when married filing a joint return. Social security is exempted, as is the first $3,000 of military and government pensions. Sales taxes are 5.75%

Corporations are taxed at a flat 9.975%. DC's corporate tax law is full of credits and deductions for various types of businesses. Perhaps because the US government is so close at hand, the state tax system is trying to out-complicate even it's big brother the IRS. DC even requires sole proprietorships to file a separate DC franchise tax return. For more information see: http://cfo.dc.gov/

Florida

There is no individual income tax in Florida. Also there is no estate tax in Florida. However there is a corporate tax- a flat 5.5%. Sales tax is set at 6% with up to 9.5% in various localities. Pass-through entities have no tax filing obligations although there is still an annual business reporting that is due- $138.75 for LLCs and $150 for corporations. Florida business portal can be viewed at: http://www.sunbiz.org/

Georgia

Personal income taxes range from 1% to 6%, the highest rate coming in at a whopping $7,000. Hey there big spender... Personal exemptions are $2,700 for single, $5,400 for married couples, and they give an extra $3,000 per dependent. The standard deduction is $2,300 for single or $3,000 for married couples, seems like a state where it pays to stay single. There is no estate tax in Georgia.

Corporations are taxed at a flat 6% in addition to an annual $50 business form filing fee. Sales tax is 4%, some localities add up to 3% more. Georgia has strong limited partnership laws where limited partners can still have some control over the business without losing their liability protection. This would be a desirable state to set up a limited partnership with a corporation as the general partner for that reason. Business information can be found at the secretary of state's site http://sos.ga.gov/index.php/ Tax information is at: https://etax.dor.ga.gov/

Hawaii

Considered one of the highest tax states, at least for individuals, Hawaii's tax rates range from 1.4% to 11%. Personal exemptions are $1144 per person, and the standard deduction is $2,200 single, $3212 for head of household, and $4,400 for married couples. Hawaii also has some very interesting credits including many energy credits, a low income housing credit, and even a credit for costs of taking care of certain types of native tree species in your yard. Film credits are refundable credits in Hawaii, making Hawaii 5-0 extra profitable for it's producers.

Estate taxes in Hawaii are especially thorny with the state taxing non-residents who own property here after the first $60,000! Non-resident estate tax rates run from 1.6%-8.4%. Residents have it a bit easier exemption wise, tax rates phase in between 3.5 million and 16 million, but the top rate is a whopping 16%. Definitely a state where estate planning is needed if you own much, especially as a non-resident.

Hawaii's corporate tax rates range from 4.5% to 6.4%, quite a bargain when compared to the individual income tax rates. Sales taxes are a reasonable 4%, up to 0.5% more in some localities. Filing corporations in Hawaii is cheap and easy- $50 fee and an online portal that walks you through the process. The annual report filing fee is also a bargain, coming in at a bank-breaking $15. Only thing is then you own a corporation in Hawaii, not exactly a state where it is easy to get business or legal processes done in general. Hawaii business registration can be found at: http://cca.hawaii.gov/breg/ The department of taxation is at: http://tax.hawaii.gov/

Idaho

Personal tax rates range from 1.6% to 7.4%. The personal exemption is a generous $3,500 for single, $7,300 for married couples, and $3,500 for each extra dependent. The standard deduction is $5,450 or double that for married couples. Idaho does not tax social security, and has many pension related exemptions. There is no estate tax in Idaho.

Corporate tax rates are a flat 7.4%, and is a rather simple and straightforward tax system as both business and personal taxes in general conform to the federal law. There are no annual fees to pay when filing the annual reports. Sales tax is 6% with some localities especially resort towns charging an extra 3%. Business tax info is available at: http://tax.idaho.gov/i-1132.cfm For forming businesses and annual report filing please see: http://sos.idaho.gov/

Illinois

Personal tax rates are a flat 5%. Exemptions are set at $2,100 per person, there is no standard deduction. Illinois does not tax distributions from any pension plans or social security, making it a good state to live in if you are going to convert an IRA to a Roth. Illinois does have an estate tax though, with a $4 million exemption.

Corporate taxes are a flat 9.5%, making S-corps and other pass-through entities look especially appealing in Illinois. Corporations must pay a $75 annual report fee, for LLCs this fee increases to $250 annually. Sales taxes are 6.25% and can be locally raised up to 10.5% Illinois tax information can be found at: http://www.revenue.state.il.us/ The Illinois Secretary of State for annual filings is located at: http://www.cyberdriveillinois.com/home.html

Indiana

Individual tax rates are a flat 3.4% with only a $1,000 deduction for single taxpayers, or double that for couples, plus and extra $1,500 for dependents. Social security tax is exempt and there is no inheritance tax.

Corporations pay a flat 7.5%, and the annual filing fee for business entities is $20. Sales tax is 7%. More information on Indiana taxes can be found at: http://www.in.gov/dor/index.htm Indiana business filing information is at: http://www.in.gov/sos/business/index.htm

Iowa

Tax rates range from 0.36% to 8.98% with the highest bracket coming into play at $67,230. Single residents have a standard deduction of $1,900, married couples get much more generous $4,760, exemptions are given as a tax credit of $40 per person. Active duty military pay is exempted. Social security and pensions are taxed but a portion may receive an exemption. While not having an estate tax, if you inherit property while living in Iowa you may face high taxes. The exemption is only $25,000 and the inheritance tax rates range from 1% to 15%.

For corporations the tax rates range from 6% to 12%. A biennial report accompanied by a $45 fee must be filed. Sales taxes are 6% with localities adding up to 2% more. Iowa business and tax information can be found at: http://www.iowa.gov/

Kansas

Tax rates range from 2.7% to 4.8% and are set to decrease each year for the next five years. Standard deduction is $4,500 or double that for married couples, and personal exemptions of $1,860 for single, $4590 for married couples and $2250 per dependent. Sales tax is 6.15%, and localities can add up to 4% more. Estate tax in Kansas has been repealed.

Corporations are taxed at 4% on the first $50,000 of income, then they pay 7% on income over that amount. Corporations and LLCs both pay a $55 annual filing fee. Kansas has a number of valuable tax credits for businesses, including an Angel Investor Credit of up to 50% of the amount of investment. More information on these credits can be seen at: http://www.ksrevenue.org/taxcredits.html For business formations and annual reports visit: https://www.kssos.org/

Kentucky

Income taxes range from 2% to 6% with a $2360 standard deduction, and an exemption credit of $20 per person. Social security and some pensions are exempt. Sales tax is a flat 6%. Kentucky has an inheritance tax, but only if the proceeds are not going to immediate family members.

Corporate tax rates range from 4% to 6%. Pass through entities are required to file a return and withhold tax on shareholders and partners payments, if tax liability appears to pass $500. There is an attractive tax credit for historic preservation available to business and real estate developers. Kentucky tax and business formation information can be found at: http://revenue.ky.gov/

Louisiana

Personal tax rates range from 2-6%, with the top rate coming in at $50,000. The standard deduction and exemption is merged to be $4,500 single or double that for married couples; an additional $1,000 is applied for each dependent. Up to $6,000 of retirement income may be excluded. Social security and most government pensions are excluded. School supplies for children and adults are a tax deduction, so save those back to school receipts.

Louisiana has high corporate tax rates ranging from 4% to 11%. In addition, a franchise tax based on capital runs at $1.50 for each $1,000 up to $300,000, then $3 per $1,000 above that. Sales taxes are 4%, but can range up to 10.75% in localities. Louisiana tax information can be seen at: http://www.rev.state.la.us/

Maine

Individual tax rates range from 2% to 7.95%, with a standard deduction of $6,100 for single filers and $10,150 for married couples. Exemptions give an extra $2,850 deduction per person. Sales tax is a flat 5.5%. Estate tax ranges from 8% to 12% on amounts in excess of $2,000,000.

Corporate tax rates range from 3.5% to 8.93%. Maine has a number of business credits available for fringe benefits and community redevelopment projects, in addition to other activities such as visual media production and fishery infrastructure improvements. Plus the Jobs and investment Credit can cover many types of businesses. Definitely worth researching if doing business in Maine. More information can be found at:

http://www.state.me.us/revenue/homepage.html

Maryland

This state is a bit complex for individual filers as not only does the state charge between 2% and 5.5%, but most of the 23 localities also charge residents between 1.15% and 3.15% as an income tax. Standard deduction is up to $2,000 for individuals and double that for married couples. An exemption amount of $3,200 per person is also allowed. Sales taxes are 6%.

All businesses, including sole proprietors, if they own any depreciable assets, must register with the Department of Assessment and Taxation and file an annual personal property return. Corporate tax is a flat 8.25%. Maryland also has many business credits. Especially interesting to note the fringe benefit credits such as the commuting credit, and the green development credits. More information on these business credits is at:

http://taxes.marylandtaxes.com/Business_Taxes/General_Info rmation/Business_Tax_Credits/

Massachusetts

Individual taxes are flat 5.5% based on the federal adjusted gross income with a personal exemption of $4,400 single, $8,800 married filing joint, and an extra $1,000 for each dependent. Social security and many government pensions are considered exempt income. State sales tax is 6.25% with many exceptions- even clothing up to $175 is exempted from sales tax. An estate tax is levied with $1 million as the exemption amount.

Corporate taxes are officially a flat 8%, but this is a bit misleading. Massachusetts has an excise tax in addition to the corporate income tax that is 9.5% of net income in addition to $2.60 per $1,000 of tangible property or net worth. The minimum excise tax is $456, plus add another $125 for filing your annual report. For LLCs there is a simpler but still relatively pricey annual filing fee of $500. Massachusetts has a voluntary disclosure program for businesses that have been engaging in business in the state but not filing taxes there that waives penalties, only valid if you are disclosing your income before receiving notification that you are in trouble. More information on all this can be found at: http://www.mass.gov/dor/

Michigan

Personal tax rates are a flat 4.25% of federal AGI with an exemption of $3,950 for single filers or $7,900 for married couples. Dependents give an extra $2,300 each. Social security and most pension income is exempt. Sales tax is a flat 6%. Michigan currently does not collect an estate tax.

Corporate taxes are a flat 6%. In addition the Single Business tax comes into pay for any business activity that earns over $350,000 in Michigan, including sales of real estate, real estate rental activities, and fees for personal services. This is a 1.9% tax that has several tax credits that can be applied toward it, but still adds up. More Michigan tax information can be found at: http://www.michigan.gov/taxes

Minnesota

Individual rates range from 5.35% to 9.85% following the federal format of obtaining taxable income almost exactly. The estate tax exemption was just raised to two million for the next five years (until 2018). The marginal tax rates were reduced and now range from 10% to 16%.

The corporate tax rate is a flat 9.8%. Sales tax is 6.875%. There also are franchise taxes, and Minnesota has a specific S-corp tax return, with minimum fees based on gross assets within the state. More Minnesota tax information can be found at:
http://www.revenue.state.mn.us/Pages/default.aspx

Mississippi

Personal tax rates fall between 3% and 5%, less a generous exemption of $6,000 if single or $12,000 if a married couple, plus another $1,500 per dependent. In addition, there is a standard deduction amount of $2,300 single or double that for married filing joint. Most retirement income is tax exempt. Sales tax is 7%. There is no functional estate tax in Mississippi.

Corporate tax rates also range from 3% to 5%. It is important to note that if you owe over $200 on corporate tax you are expected to make estimated payments. There also is a franchise tax computed on $2.50 of each $1,000 of capital employed and assessed value of property in your business, with a $25 minimum fee. More tax and business information can be found at: http://www.dor.ms.gov/

Missouri

Individual taxes span the distance from 1% to 6%, with the highest rate coming in at a grandiose $9,000. Standard deduction is $6,100 for the single crowd, or double that for married couples filing together. Exemptions are $2,100 single, $4,200 married, and an extra $1,200 per dependent. A deduction for how much federal tax was paid is also taken. Social security is mostly exempt, and a portion of some pensions are. Sales taxes are 4.225%. There is no estate tax in Missouri.

Corporate tax rates are a flat 6.25%. Franchise taxes are only due if assets are over one million dollars. The franchise tax, if due, is 1/150th of 1% (0.000067). For more information please see: http://www.dor.mo.gov/

Montana

Tax rates range from 1% to 6.9% for individuals with the highest bracket coming in at $15,600. Standard deductions are $4,200 single, or double that for married couples. An exemption of $2,140 per person is given. All retirement income is taxable. There is no sales tax or estate tax.

Corporate tax rates are 6.75%. Personal service businesses, contractors, and lodging facilities have additional income taxes levied on them. More tax information can be found at: http://revenue.mt.gov/

Nebraska

Individual taxpayers fall into tax brackets ranging from 2.56% to 6.84%, with the highest bracket coming in around $27,000. Standard deduction is $5,450 and double that for married couples. In addition, a tax credit of $120 per person is taken out. Social security and pensions are taxable the same as how the federal taxes them. Nebraska's estate tax has been repealed. Sales tax is 5.5% but localities can add up to 2% additional on top of that.

Corporate tax rates range from 5.58% to 7.81%. In addition an annual benefit report must be filed that costs $25 plus $5 per page for recording costs. For more information on business requirements please visit: http://www.sos.ne.gov/dyindex.html for tax information: http://www.revenue.nebraska.gov/index.html

Nevada

Nevada has no personal income tax. There is a sales tax of 6.875%, and counties may add another 1.25%. There is no estate tax.

There is no corporate tax in Nevada. There is, however, an annual list filing fee that ranges from $125 to $11,100 depending on the value of capitalized shares. Therefore, be sure to give your shares very low value if forming in Nevada. LLCs also pay a $125 annual filing fee for listing their member names. Both corps and LLC's are subject to a $200 annual business license fees. While Nevada corporations are gaining popularity, Nevada likely leads the US in LLC filings with it's clearly written LLC laws. More information on business formation in Nevada can be found at: http://nvsos.gov/index.aspx?page=4

Tax Tip: In states like Nevada and Delaware that charge and annual franchise tax based on share capitalization value it pays off when forming the business to have a $0.001 or even $0.0001 share value.

New Hampshire

New Hampshire only levies a tax on dividend and interest income- a flat 5% on any amount over $2,400. Not good news for S-corp owners in the state as most S-corp income is distributed as a dividend. There is no estate tax in New Hampshire.

Corporate tax rates are a flat 8.5%. Annual report fees for an LLC or Corporation run $800. There is no across the board sales tax, but there is a 9% tax on restaurant meals. For more tax information please see: http://www.revenue.nh.gov/

New Jersey

New Jersey tax rates range from 1.4% to 8.94% for individual filers. The top tax rate doesn't come into play until $500,000 of income is reached. Only a $1,000 per person exemption is given, no standard deduction. Social security is not taxable, but pensions are.

New Jersey has an inheritance tax- meaning if you are given or bequested real property worth more than $500 the state wants you to pay somewhere between 11% and 16% of the value to them. Ouch! New Jersey also has a separate estate tax on estates valued greater than $675,000.

New Jersey also charges a tax on partnerships, based on a per partner fee. Corporate taxes are a flat 9% with a $500 minimum tax. More New Jersey tax information can be found at: http://www.state.nj.us/treasury/taxation/index.shtml

New Mexico

Individual rates range from 1.7% to 4.9%, standard deductions and exemptions are the same as federal, retired taxpayers have additional exemptions, can be more than double the standard amount. One of the four states that makes it difficult to move abroad. They consider those who move overseas still residents unless they have fully severed ties within the state. An inheritance may be included in modified adjusted gross income and taxed that way, but there is no specific inheritance or estate tax.

Corporate taxes range from 4.8% to 7.3%. Sales tax is set a 5.125% but cities and counties may add an additional 6.625%. New Mexico also charges businesses a 5.3% annual excise tax on use of goods and services. More information on New

Mexico taxes can be viewed at:
http://www.tax.newmexico.gov/

New York

Personal tax rates range from 4% to 8.82%. Standard deduction is $7,500, double if a married couple, and dependents contribute another $4,000 each. New York City also has an income tax. New York has an estate tax over $1 million if the decedent is a US citizen, or if a non-citizen only if they need to file an estate tax. Talk about trying to give people a reason to surrender citizenship!

However, for lower income taxpayers there are a number of valuable credits. This includes refundable child and dependent care credits, the empire state credit and even a NY earned income credit! There are additional credits for New York City residents as well.

Corporate tax in the big apple is a flat rate 7.1%. Sales taxes state-wide are only 4% but cities and counties can add up to 5% more. There are a range of business credits available as well- ranging from film credits to solar installation and more. For more information on NY taxes you may view: http://www.tax.ny.gov/

North Carolina

Starting in 2015, North Carolina will have a flat tax rate of 5.75%. Standard deduction is $3,000, or double when married, exemptions are $1,200 for single or $2,500 if married. No additional is given for dependents. Sales tax is 4.75%, but counties and cities can charge 2-3% more. The estate tax in North Carolina has been instituted and repealed several times. Currently there is no estate tax.

The corporate income tax rate is a flat 6.9%. North Carolina also imposes a franchise tax of $1.50 per $1,000. For more information please see: http://www.dor.state.nc.us/

North Dakota

Individual tax rates range from 1.22% to 3.22%, exemption and standard deduction amounts are the same as the federal, plus North Dakota offers a marriage credit. Sales taxes are 5%, but cities and counties can tack on an additional 3%. No estate tax is due regardless of the estate's value, but an estate tax return must be filed nonetheless.

Corporate taxes range from 1.48% to 4.53%, financial institutions are levied an additional tax. For additional information you may view: http://www.nd.gov/tax/

Ohio

Personal tax rates are between 0.587% and 5.421%, exemptions are $1,700 per person, no standard deduction is given. Social security is exempt and pensioners receive some additional tax credits. Sales tax is 5.5%, and cities and counties may levy an additional 2.25%. There is no estate tax in Ohio.

Corporate income taxes were repealed, but many corporations are still subject to the Commercial Activities Tax based on gross receipts. For more information on this and other business taxes in Ohio please see: http://www.tax.ohio.gov/commercial_activities.aspx

Oklahoma

Individual tax rates range from 0.5% to 5.25%, with the highest bracket coming in at $8,701. Standard deduction is $5,950 single and $11,900 married, with an additional $1,000 exemption per person. Oklahoma does not currently collect an estate tax.

Corporations are taxed at a flat 6%. Oklahoma also charges a franchise tax of $1.25 per every $1,000 of assets in the state. Sales taxes are state-wide 4.5%, but cities can add up to 2% additional if they so desire. For more information please see: http://www.tax.ok.gov/

Oregon

Individual rates range from 5% to 9.90%. There is no sales tax in Oregon. An estate tax applies to estates valued at $1 million or more.

Corporate tax rates range from 6.6% to 7.6%, with a minimum tax of $150. Oregon also has a personal property excise tax on businesses. For more information please visit the Oregon department of revenue at: http://www.oregon.gov/dor/Pages/index.aspx

Pennsylvania

With a 3.07% flat rate income tax, Pennsylvania is one of the lower taxed states income-wise. But there are no exemptions or deductions given so this flat tax is levied from the first dollar. Pennsylvania has no estate tax, but it has an inheritance tax of 4.5% when property is passed parents to children, 12% to siblings and 15% to all other heirs.

Corporations are taxed at a flat 9.99% and the rules are rather straightforward. Sales tax is 6% but localities may add another 2%. For more detailed information please see: http://www.revenue.state.pa.us/

Rhode Island

Tax rates have been lowered recently in Rhode Island, with the new top rate being 5.75%, and the lowest rate is

3.75%. Sales taxes come in at 7%. Rhode Island charges an estate tax, the current exemption is $921,655 for 2014.

The corporate tax rate has also just been cut- to 7% down from 9%, this takes effect starting in the tax year January 1, 2015. The franchise tax has also recently been repealed. With all these changes, Rhode Island is in the process of making itself a much more business friendly state. However, S-corps are still caught in the middle of the law changes with a $500 minimum tax. For more information you may see: http://www.tax.state.ri.us/

South Carolina

Taxes range from 3% to 5% for individuals. Standard deductions and exemptions along lines of the federal are used. South Carolina is one of the four states that makes it difficult to move abroad. They consider those who move out of the state still residents unless they have fully severed ties, and will hunt residents down the world over demanding tax due. Sales tax is 6% but may be up to 3% more in certain counties. There is no estate tax in South Carolina.

Corporations pay a flat tax of 5%. Many valuable tax credits are available, including a credit for developing corporate headquarters in South Carolina, and an abandoned buildings revitalization credit. For more information on taxation please see: http://www.sctax.org/default.htm

South Dakota

There is no individual or corporate income tax in South Dakota. There is a sales tax of 4% and municipalities may add up to 2.75% additional. There are no estate taxes. For more information on forming South Dakota businesses you may visit: https://sdsos.gov/business-services/default.aspx

Tennessee

Only dividends and interest are taxed in Tennessee, wages and other earned income are not. An inheritance tax ranges from 5.5% to 9.5% of the value of the inherited property. Sales taxes are 7% but may be up to 2.75% higher in various localities.

There is a corporate flat tax rate of 6.5%, there also is a franchise tax that is rather complex to determine, as it taxes various assets at differing rates. For more information please see: http://www.tn.gov/revenue/

Texas

Texas has no personal income tax. Sales taxes are 6.25% and can go up to 8.25% in various municipalities. There also is no estate tax.

Corporations don't have a tax, per se. However, there is a franchise tax that applies to all business entities- including partnerships, joint ventures and single member LLCs. For more information on who is taxed please see: http://www.window.state.tx.us/taxinfo/franchise/faq_tax_ent.html

Utah

Individual taxpayers pay a flat rate tax of 5%, with an exemption amount of $2,850 per person. There is no standard deduction. Sales taxes are set at 5.95% for the state, but local options may raise the tax rate another 5% or so. There is no estate tax in Utah.

Corporate taxes also fall under the very fairly meted out 5% flat tax. There is a minimum $100 tax, but this does not apply to S-corps. For more information please visit: http://tax.utah.gov/

Vermont

Individual tax rates range from 3.55% to 8.95%, after taking out a $3,900 per person exemption. Sales taxes are 6%, and local areas can add another 1%. Vermont has a tax on estates valued over $2,750,000.

Corporate tax rates range from 6% to 8.5%. There also is a business entity minimum tax of $250 that applies to Partnerships, LLCs and S-corps. More information can be found at: http://www.state.vt.us/tax/index.shtml

Virginia

Personal tax rates range from 2% to 5.75% after allotting for a standard deduction of $3,000 for single taxpayers and double that for married couples, plus an exemption of $930 per person. Virginia is one of the four states that makes it difficult to move abroad. They consider those who move out of the state still residents unless they have fully severed ties. Sales tax is 5.3% in most areas, a few localities bring it up to 7%. There is no estate tax in Virginia.

There is a flat 6% corporate tax. There are no minimum taxes, but the late filing fees are extremely heavy ($200 per month for the first six months) so be sure in this state that you file extensions and returns on time. More information on taxation in Virginia can be found at: http://www.tax.virginia.gov/

Washington

There is no personal income tax in Washington. State sales taxes are 6.5% and may jump to 9.5% depending on the locality. There is an estate tax with a $2 million exemption amount.

There is technically no corporate income tax in Washington. However, it has a Business and Occupation tax which essentially is an income tax based on gross receipts rather than net. Tax rates can be found at: http://dor.wa.gov/Content/FindTaxesAndRates/BAndOTax/BandOrates.aspx

West Virginia

Tax rates range from 3% to 6.5% for individuals. No standard deduction is given, but an exemption of $2,000 per person is allowed. There is no estate tax in West Virginia. There is a 6% sales tax, and a few localities tack another 1% on.

Corporations are taxed at a flat rate of 6.5%. There also is a franchise tax that charges $0.55 per $100 of taxable capital with a minimum tax of $50. For more information please see: http://www.wva.state.wv.us/wvtax/WestVirginiaStateTaxDepartment.aspx

Wisconsin

Individual tax rates vary from 4.6% to 6.65%. There is a rather complex formula to determine taxable income using tax tables for figuring standard deductions and exemptions. There currently is no estate tax in Wisconsin.

Corporate tax rates are 7.9% flat. Sales tax is officially 5% but most counties add an additional 1.5% on top of that. For more information please see: http://revenue.wi.gov/

Wyoming

It is a toss up if Wyoming or Nevada have lower taxes, they both seem to be competing for the most tax friendly states. There is no personal or corporate income tax in Wyoming, and no estate tax. There is a state sales tax of 4%.

For more information on tax in Wyoming you can go to: http://revenue.wyo.gov/

Chapter 13: Keeping Balance

The Importance of Balance

Balance sheets are important to running a business, giving a snapshot into the financial health of your enterprise. Balance sheets are frequently required for borrowing funds, and it is good to prepare personal balance sheets every so often as well so as to know where your overall investments stand.

The balance sheet is one of the more often overlooked elements of tax preparation, and is not required for partnerships or corporations with gross income under $250,000 and assets under $250,000 for corporations or $1,000,000 for partnerships, yet another reason to own real estate in an LLC and never in a corporate structure. Businesses with over $10,000,000 in assets must file form M-3 instead, but as that likely has little bearing on most of the readers of this book I will stick to covering the basic balance sheet concepts.

> *Tax Tip: Year-end balances one year must always be the starting year balances the next.*

Assets

The top half of the balance sheet is what is considered assets, or positive elements of what the business owns. The main items that go in here are cash, amounts due to the business, and physical goods and property owned less any depreciation amounts. Intangibles such as goodwill or intellectual property that has been purchased can also show up on the top of the balance sheet.

Values of property such as real estate or vehicles is reduced by depreciation amounts with the asset side. Biological assets such as trees and farm animals can also be listed here. Intangible assets such as patents and trademarks or goodwill from purchasing a business also go in the asset category.

Liabilities

The lower half of the balance sheet contains liabilities, or what the company owes to others. This lower half must balance with the top half and end in the same amount, which is why it is known as a balance sheet. This lower half includes liabilities such as loans the company owes to others, and retained earnings.

For tax purposes, the liabilities section also contains shareholder equity or capital contributions. This can be a tricky balance sheet subject. Once forming a corporation shareholders cannot just contribute capital into the company.

Capital contributions must either be in the form of issues of additional stock in exchange for capital contributed, or as loans from shareholders.

Chapter 14: World Wide Tax

International Tax Strategies

Let me start this chapter with a big warning- if you do not have legitimate business reasons for forming a business abroad, there is a high likelihood that any tax advantages you gain by having an overseas company will be disallowed. Examples of legitimate reasons for having a foreign corporation include the following: founders who live overseas, the majority of the business is international in scope, or there are foreign investors.

I'm including this chapter here because many people these days do travel and live internationally (I do and have) and there are some who may legally benefit from the information here. But also I'm including it as a warning to not get caught up in the idea of moving your firm to the Cayman's or British Virgin Islands on the advice of some spinster. Unless you have legitimate business reasons to do so it will not hold water and you will end up drowning in penalties and interest, not to mention the legal fees these so-called "experts" charge for their bad advice.

Also moving overseas does not mean you are suddenly free of U.S. taxes. Uncle Sam requires all citizens and green card holders to continue to file U.S. taxes after moving abroad. Yet, thanks to the foreign earned income exclusion and the credit for foreign taxes, expatriates often don't have a dime of tax liability. Filing is still important though. Ranging beyond the risk of penalties and interest, residents can be denied renewal of their green card by neglecting to file, and citizens can have a difficult time passing their citizenship on to children born abroad or getting visas for loved ones.

First I will start with the individual aspects of foreign income- the foreign earned income exclusion (Form 2555), foreign tax credit (Form 1116) and international totalization agreements. Then I will touch on the business aspects such as Form 5471.

Foreign Earned Income Exclusion (Form 2555)

With the foreign earned income exclusion you may be able to exclude $97,600 worth of taxable income for 2013. Keep in mind though that this only applies to income earned in a foreign country. If you earn income within the U.S. while living overseas, including interest and retirement income, you will still be taxed on that income as if you were living in the U.S.

> *Tax Tip: It is advantageous to pay yourself wages if you own a foreign company as wages are excluded- whereas dividends are not.*

On wages there is no requirement to pay into any social security system either. You also may exclude income earned in a business from either being self-employed or a partner in a partnership. However, this income may be subject to self-employment tax if you don't pay into your resident country's social security system and your resident country has a tax treaty with the US. We will discuss this under international totalization agreements later in this chapter.

To qualify for the foreign earned income exclusion one of two tests must be met- the bonafide residence test or the physical presence test. In general, the physical presence test is preferable as it is easier to qualify for, only requiring that you have lived in a foreign country for 330 days out of a 12 month period, and the dates may be adjusted throughout the year prior and following to meet this requirement. For example, if you moved abroad in November your twelve months could start in October and continue to the end of September the following year. In this situation you would need to file an extension and wait to file until you have been in the country for the full period before filing your taxes. By adjusting the calendar year this may also allow some earned income to flow through allowing one to qualify for IRA contributions and child tax credit, when applicable.

When a taxpayer has been in the US for more than 35 days in the year however, the bonafide residence test must be used. This qualifies one based on far more intrusive questions, such as: visa status, if family members live with you, and if you keep up a house in the US. To qualify for the bonafide residence test you must also have lived overseas for at least one full calendar year.

In addition to the foreign earned income exclusion you also may claim an exclusion for foreign housing costs up to $15,616 in 2013. It is important to note that housing expenses must be paid out of pocket, not by your employer or reimbursed. Married couples can only claim one foreign housing exclusion, unless the spouses maintain two separate homes not within reasonable commuting distance of one another.

One important aspect of the foreign earned income exclusion is you cannot use it one year, then switch to the foreign tax credit the next, then back to the earned income exclusion. Once you elect to forego it you lost the exclusion for a number of future years. Therefore it is always good to check the first year you would file this if the foreign tax credit would also wipe out tax liability. If so, this is advantageous as the foreign tax credit often will have a carryover amount that can be used in future years.

Also it is important to note that filing Form 2555 excludes you from claiming the earned income credit, rarely an issue as in order to claim that a child must have lived with you in the US for at least half the year. Still, worth noting.

Foreign Tax Credit (Form 1116)

Preventing double taxation, the foreign tax credit and deduction allows you to offset your U.S. taxes with the taxes you paid to other countries. But no double-dipping. You can't take a foreign tax credit or deduction for amounts you excluded from income with the foreign earned income or housing exclusions.

Probably one of the more misunderstood credits in the tax code, many preparers simply forego filing the 1116 at all as generally the cost they must charge for filing the form is greater than the benefit the client will receive. In general, the amount of foreign tax credit available is often very small compared to what has been paid as this is limited by other deductions, such as a portion of the standard deduction and exemptions related to the income this is based on.

The foreign tax credit must also be broken out based on types of income. Therefore I often have foreign clients filing three forms 1116 in a single tax return. The first category of income most commonly used is general income, or income earned in a foreign country as wages, business income or a pension. Income Re-sourced by Treaty, or income that is U.S. sourced but has been taxed in the foreign country because of a tax treaty. The third common category is passive income, or income from interest, dividends, capital gains, royalties and real estate.

The foreign tax credit forms must be carefully prepared to exempt any U.S. deductions related to this income such as the earned income exclusion or adjustments for student loan interest payments, moving expenses, or half of the Self-employment tax. As this is a very complex area of tax law, and an easy one to make mistakes in, if this is something that relates to your income I would highly suggest working with a tax preparer who is an expert in this area of practice.

International Totalization Agreements

Tax treaties, and the tax exemptions they include, are a relatively new area of tax law, most treaties being less than 30 years old and commonly misunderstood. If you live in a foreign country I would suggest reading the totalization agreement relating to your country in full.

In order to make use of this exemption you must include a statement in the return referring to the agreement. If you are audited the IRS will request a letter on the official letterhead of the social security office in your resident country showing that you have indeed paid into the system for x number of years.

Countries with Social Security Agreeements	Date of Entry into Force
Italy	November 1, 1978
Germany	December 1, 1979
Switzerland	November 1, 1980
Belgium	July 1, 1984
Norway	July 1, 1984
Canada	August 1, 1984
United Kingdom	January 1, 1985
Sweden	January 1, 1987
Spain	April 1, 1988
France	July 1, 1988
Portugal	August 1, 1989
Netherlands	November 1, 1990
Austria	November 1, 1991
Finland	November 1, 1992
Ireland	September 1, 1993
Luxembourg	November 1, 1993
Greece	September 1, 1994
South Korea	April 1, 2001
Chile	December 1, 2001
Australia	October 1, 2002
Japan	October 1, 2005

Denmark	October 1, 2008
Czech Republic	January 1, 2009
Poland	March 1, 2009
Slovak Republic	May 1, 2014

State Tax Issues

One thing many expats overlook is state tax requirements. Every state has their own regulations regarding residency, and many states continue to demand tax from expats who have moved abroad. The four states that typically present challenges for expats are: California, New Mexico, South Carolina, and Virginia. In these states, you must prove to the government that you are breaking ties with your hometown and have no intention of moving back. Proving this can be difficult. Regardless of the state, the best way to cut ties is to close all financial accounts and to use a mailing address overseas or in a tax-free state.

Totally Tax-Free Life

There are fifteen countries worldwide which have no income tax whatsoever: Monaco, Andorra, Kuwait, U.A.E., Qatar, Oman, Brunei, Bermuda, British Virgin Islands, Bahamas, Cayman Islands, Anguilla, Turks and Caicos, Maldives, and Vanuatu. Paired with the foreign earned income exclusion, living a life in one of those havens may have you living tax free for good.

Even on a remote island paradise though there is no escaping taxes, or at least filing the paperwork. Taxpayers who live outside of the U.S. and Puerto Rico must file a tax return or extension by June 15th of each year.

You could always give up your U.S. citizenship or residency, but in that case you still are required to file a form 1040NR reporting your income and assets for each of the next ten years, in addition to other complications that make this not worthwhile for most. Filing might be a necessary evil, but at least with the exclusions and credits a large portion of expatriates don't have to pay any U.S. taxes.

Links:

For more information on the foreign earned income exclusion and credit for foreign taxes paid view the IRS' Pub 54:
http://www.irs.gov/pub/irs-pdf/p54.pdf

http://www.ssa.gov/international/agreements_overview.html
http://www.ssa.gov/international/status.html

Chapter 15: Tax Shelters

Disclosed Positions

My mom used to tell me growing up that in life there is very little right and wrong, no absolute black and white, just many varying shades of grey. In tax law this is true more than anywhere else, it is all good or bad depending on the perspective it is viewed from. Nothing is set in stone, it all depends on the relationship to the business relevance of a deduction. And even the most legal ways of "saving" on taxes can be disallowed if they are used for purposes of "avoiding" taxes. Semantics means everything in this game.

These grey areas I will cover in this chapter are just a few of many of the real aggressive positions that can be taken on a tax return. Most of them are involving the related party rules and fringe benefits, where it is recognized that they may or may not be allowed. Declaring these transactions is to some degree like waving a big sign saying, "audit me". Therefore, a reserve is required to be set aside in case the position is disallowed. I don't recommend using disclosed positions, unless you are a huge multinational corporation where the benefits are large enough to warrant the hassle of having your financial details closely examined. Often I wonder if even in those cases, disclosed positions are mainly of benefit to the accountants who have work security for a couple years worth of audits. There are so many legal ways to save on taxes it just seems unnecessary, and frankly, greedy, to file these positions in all but the most unusual of cases.

But it is good to have some idea of what these transactions may be, so as to prevent getting unwaringly duped into filing one, and the tax consequences that will follow. Also I have added a link at the end of the chapter to the IRS's web page where they list the tax shelters they have recently determined and are going after.

Large Business or Currency Losses

If, for individuals, you have losses of more than $2 million in a single year or $4 million spread over several years, or for corps $10 million/$20 million respectfully, then you must file form 8886 to disclose the transaction. This does not refer to losses on real estate, casualty or theft losses or certain other transactions.

Intermediary Transactions

This is when shareholders of a corporation with built in gains sell off their interests to a third controlled corporation, in order to get transfer ownership and reduce the amount of built in gains. Then, the intermediary company can sell the assets and have lower reportable gains than the previous shareholders. Sneaky sneaky... and obviously something that on closer glance could be disallowed. A good example of the types of transactions that "if they sound too good to be true..." well you get the idea.

This also includes complex transactions using installment method and spreading basis between multiple companies.

There is a well known tax court case discussing this issue, the ASA Investerings Partnership case, link provided at the end of the chapter.

Inflated Basis Transactions

A number of reportable tax positions involve various ploys to artificially increase basis by borrowing against assets or claiming losses for capital outlays that have been recovered. Basically there is no free lunch, and all these complicated transactions get caught eventually. The only one who really makes money off them is the whistle-blower, who gets 15-30% of the taxes and penalties collected. Wonder if anyone has set up a fake tax shelter scam yet just to report people, only a matter of time before that scam happens. The bottom line is, clever accountants will continue to come up with slightly different variations on these tax schemes for a long time to come, best just to avoid anything that sounds too easy. Just a good reminder that tax planning must be done all along, not as a band-aid measure at the end.

Sale of Charitable Remainder Trust Assets

Setting up a trust to benefit your favorite charity can still be a wise tax move, but the types of transactions you make may now be subject to added scrutiny. Basically a trust is formed and created in such a way where the sale of appreciated assets funds an annuity of sort for the grantor or other beneficiary then designates a charity as the remainder beneficiary. Grantor receives a charitable donation based on the Fair Market Value of the contributed assets on formation of the trust, and has taxable income from the annuity. So far all legal, and very tax beneficial. The trouble comes in if the trust sells the new assets to another company, then dissolves the trust. The sale of the new assets at fair market value has nearly no gain as those assets were recently purchased at fair market value, and the grantor when receiving the assets back is taxed at the new rate of gain, or very little. The charity gets nothing.

While this type of maneuvering is technically legal, it is an example of creating a transaction that violates the intention of a law. If it can be tied to the intention of being done in order to avoid taxes, then it can be redetermined as being an illegal transaction and the full amount of gain on the initial assets will be considered taxable.

> *Tax Tip: The difference between what is legal and illegal is often only the intention from which the transaction was entered into. Documenting this is paramount to making a deduction stick.*

Once too many people take part in a transaction such as this, the positive aspects of a legal loophole like charitable remainder trusts will be forgotten, and new laws enacted to make forming or managing such a trust more difficult and less beneficial. Such is the lifecycle of tax planning tools from helpful tax planning opportunity, to abused tax shelter.

Links:

IRS list of recognized and abusive tax transactions that must be listed:
http://www.irs.gov/Businesses/Corporations/Listed-Transactions---LB&I-Tier-I-Issues

IRS website on the most recently identified tax shelters:
http://www.irs.gov/Businesses/Corporations/Abusive-Tax-Sh
elters-and-Transactions

The ASA Investerings Partnership case 98-1583:
http://www.irs.gov/Businesses/Corporations/Listed-Transact
ions---LB&I-Tier-I-Issues

Chapter 16: Tax Payments

Death and Taxes

Tax payments. Like the old cliche goes, the two things in life you can't escape are death and paying taxes. We do whatever we can first to find ways to minimize this amount, but sometimes the inevitable is all that is left. When faced with a bill it's good to remember the positive side, it is better to make money and pay taxes then not to make money at all. And it is better to pay ahead of time, than to get a whole lot of penalties and interest tacked on. We will go into the consequences of non-payment here, but hopefully that won't apply in your case.

When is this tax really due?

Probably earlier than you think. Even though there are extensions available to stretch filing out to October 15th for individuals, or September 15th for business entities, the tax owed is still considered due on April 15th. If you don't pay the tax owed by that deadline you will face a ½ of 1 percent penalty for each month the tax is overdue, maxing out at 25%.

Failure to file penalties are even worse, that is why it is important to file that extension even if you don't know what you will pay yet. The failure-to-file penalty is a hefty 5% monthly, also capped at 25%. If you filed an extension by April 15th and made at least 90% of your tax due as a payment then you will not face any penalties by not paying the remaining balance due until you file before the extended deadline of April 15th.

The IRS also charges interest on payments due, but their rate is a relative bargain compared to the penalties. The interest rate is the prime federal short term rate plus 3%. This is updated quarterly, and when they determine interest due they use daily compounding. Because of these factors it is generally better to allow the IRS to figure interest. From experience, it tends to come out as less owed when the IRS figures it than when I use tax software to try and determine it. See the IRS is really kind and generous after all.

Estimated Payments

Once you have ended up owing taxes on year you are expected by the government to anticipate this in future years and pay in quarterly as taxes are not actually due at the end of the year, but in the quarter directly after they are earned. This is why when you work a job your employer holds payroll taxes out from your paycheck, then pays them in at the end of the quarter to be your withholding towards the tax year. When you are self-employed or own a business you are expected to do this yourself. So as not not pay penalties, estimated taxes must be based either on 100% of your prior year's tax owed or 90% of the projected amount you will owe the next year. This amount is divided in four and payed on the following dates: April 15th, July 15th, October 15th and January 15th. If you miss one then just double up on the next.

> *Tax Tip: When sending estimated payments in, send the envelopes through certified mail, or pay via the IRS' online payment system to make certain your payment is received.*

The link for making online payments is provided at the end of the chapter. I've had a number of clients who have had the IRS lose their checks and never cash them, leaving them a mess of letters to send off trying to minimize penalties after filing. A big hassle that is easy to avoid with a little pre-planning and common sense.

Important Tax Dates

Be aware that if any of the due dates listed below fall on a weekend or holiday the due date will be the following business day.

January 1st	Start of the Calendar Year
January 15th	4th Quarter Estimated Payment Due
January 31st	Send forms W-2 and 1099 to workers
January 31st	File form 941 or 944 for payroll taxes
January 31st	File form 940 for unemployment taxes
February 28th	Form 1099, W-2G and 1098 Paper Filing Deadline
March 15th	Corporation Tax Returns or Extensions Due

March 31st	Form 1099, W-2G and 1098 E-filing Deadline
April 15th	Individual Tax Returns or Extensions Due
April 15th	Partnership Tax Returns or Extensions Due
April 15th	Prior Tax Year Additional Payments Due
April 15th	1st Estimated Payment Due
April 30th	Pay first quarter federal unemployment taxes
April 30th	File form 941 reporting first quarter payroll taxes
June 15th	Foreign Resident Tax Returns or Extensions Due
June 30th	FBAR Reports Final Deadline
July 15th	2nd Quarter Estimated Payment Due
July 31st	File form 941 reporting second quarter payroll taxes
July 31st	Pay second quarter federal unemployment taxes
September 15th	Partnership and Corporation Tax Return Final Deadline
October 15th	Individual Tax Return Final Deadline
October 15th	3rd Quarter Estimated Payment Due
October 31st	File form 941 reporting third quarter payroll taxes

| October 31st | Pay third quarter federal unemployment taxes |

When to Pay Payroll Taxes

Less than $2500 per quarter	submit amounts due on form 941 with your timely filed return
Up to $50,000 in "look-back period"*	deposits are paid the 15th of each month for the payroll up to the end of the prior month
From $50,000 to $100,000 in "look-back period"*	semi weekly deposits paid on Wednesday or Friday depending on payroll pay day
Over $100,000 in "look-back period"	next-day deposits are required

*"look-back period" refers to year before June 30th.

Links:

IRS Payments: http://www.irs.gov/Payments

Chapter 17: Looking Forward

Decisions are Key

The road to tax troubles is paved with bad investment decisions. Tax shelters seem like an easy way out, but the truth is that the decisions needed to make for good tax planning should be made when assets are purchased, not sold. Please keep in mind that I am not a licensed investment advisor, what I state in this chapter is my own opinion on investment matters formed from experience, a tax preparer's view of investing you could say. My goal isn't to tell you what to invest in, but perhaps to give you a few new questions to ask your investment advisor before making new decisions.

Investment Choices

When I was saving to buy my first house, I quadrupled my investment by leveraging my money in the stock market. How did I do this? Very carefully. First timing was on my side- I risked everything and put my entire $5,000 savings into stocks after September 11, 2001. Seeing the stock market drop a huge amount when it resumed trading I started searching for firms I thought were undervalued, and bought them. I picked a few mediocre companies that never amounted to much and a couple stars that had huge gains. Sold from the ones that had done poorly and put more into the stars, reinvesting and reaping in gains until I was ready to buy my house.

So one may ask, if I did it then why not stay with it? The truth is, it takes a tremendous amount of time and effort to profit off stocks. Most people lose money or barely earn anything. I'd say somewhere between 3 and 5% of the clients I see in the tax business actually make more than 6% between dividends and capital gains on their stock investments. The remainder barely earn enough to cover the fees the investment companies make for churning their portfolios. Then the earnings of any gains are taxed, lowering further any real gains, and creating a growth hurdle the new investments must surpass in order to make a profit. Foreign mutual funds are even worse for American investors. With the mark-to-market rules these accounts are taxed at short term capital gains rates when they go up in value, and no deduction if they lose value, and that is the best tax treatment option available for most.

Real estate can be a good investment if you have the time and inclination to find good deals, and deal with the management issues. But it can also be illiquid during a down market and rental hassles can outweigh any gains when the true time investment is figured in. Still, few investments pack the potential overall gains that rental properties can have. About half of the very wealthy people I know made at least a good portion of their fortunes through real estate investment or development.

Tax-exempt bonds can be a good investment, the rates of return on them are typically better than treasury rates and they are nearly as safe. There is risk of default however, so check out the municipality carefully. Also the coupon values can get ravaged by rising interest rates. Still, they are a good value, and something nearly all of my billionaire friends have most of their liquid assets invested in right now.

Retirement Planning

I would assume that everyone who would get this far into a book on small business income taxes, already knows a good bit about 401k plans and IRAs. So many books and articles are written on retirement planning, that I don't want to go into it too deeply. However, it deserves some mention, as socking away pre-tax money to grow in tax-deferred ways should have a place in your overall financial plan, and can be an easy way to save on taxes.

IRA's come in two flavors- traditional and Roth. Traditional can be contributed to with either pre tax or after tax dollars. If it is considered pre-tax, then there is an adjustment to income on the front page of the 1040. Distributions from traditional IRAs are considered ordinary income when received, and any non-deductible contributions become basis that should be kept track of as it will not be taxable when distributed. Roth IRAs are contributed to with after tax dollars, and the big advantage is that distributions are tax free when received. There are limits to who can contribute to a Roth, for 2014 if you are single or head of household filing status, the amount you can contribute begins to phase out at $114,000 and is gone at $129,000, for those filing married filing joint, the limits are $181,000/$191,000 respectively, and for married filing separate, contributions are only allowed if AGI is less than $10,000.

To contribute to any IRA, you must have earned income at least equal to the amount of contribution. Traditional IRA's can be deductible without any income limits as long as neither you nor your spouse (if applicable) are covered by a retirement plan at work. This often is a better decision for taxpayers who earn more than the Roth limits or otherwise expect their income to be lower upon retirement, particularly those who are near retirement age. Traditional IRAs can be converted to Roths, but it is important to keep in mind that this whole amount will be considered taxable income in the year it is converted, raising your gross income so your overall tax bracket may be significantly higher.

Self-directed IRA accounts are worth mentioning. These can be good to invest beyond brokerage assets into real estate and pretty much anything you could imagine investing in. There are some potential issues with closely related transactions though, loaning money to yourself or your business not allowable. It seems only too obvious to me, but remember to buy assets that would be more highly taxed in your deferred growth plan. I've seen clients owning tax-exempt bonds in IRA accounts more times than I want to remember.

If you own a business entity you have further retirement contribution options that may include SEP-IRAs, Keough IRAs and 401ks if you own a corporation. These all have higher contribution limits than individual IRA accounts, therefore more pre-tax money can be socked away into tax deferred accounts. Win-win.

Estate Taxes

The estate tax exemption amounts continue to be indexed upwards, $5,340,000 for 2014. In addition, there is now a ruling that a surviving spouse can add the decedent spouse's exemption to their own, leveraging that amount for a married couple upwards of $10,680,000. For those who need planning beyond this amount, there are many clever strategies out there to legally work magic, such as forming a charitable remainder trust, as I touched on in chapter 15.

Also keep state taxes in mind as many states have low exemption estate or inheritance taxes that can make planning worthwhile still even though the federal estate taxes are so favorable now. In chapter 12 where we looked at state taxes, we covered what these amounts are on a state by state basis.

Gift Taxes

As with the inheritance tax, the gift tax exclusion amount continues to rise, although not increasing very much. The current annual exclusion amount is $14,000, if you give money to anyone in amounts higher than this you as the donor may be subject to filing a gift tax return. You have a credit for your full basic credit amount, which is the same amount as in the estate tax exemption listed above, meaning you likely will not pay tax on this gift.

One important issue to note, is that if you do make gifts do not give away appreciated property that you have a low basis in, such as a home. Upon your death, if a family member receives your home it's basis will be the same as fair market value, and this will also be it's value in the estate. If you give a home away your general credit will still be reduced by the amount relating to fair market value, but the recipient of the gift will receive your basis in the property- meaning when they sell it they will have to pay tax on the gain that was already included as taxable in your estate, not a good deal.

Resources

IRS Information

Internal Revenue Service. (2014). *Online Ordering for Information Returns and Employer Returns.* Available: http://www.irs.gov/Businesses/Online-Ordering-for-Information-Returns-and-Employer-Returns. Last accessed 23rd Aug 2014.

Internal Revenue Service. (2014). *Publication 15 Cat. No. 10000W (Circular E), Employer's Tax Guide.* Available: http://www.irs.gov/pub/irs-pdf/p15.pdf. Last accessed 23rd Aug 2014.

Internal Revenue Service. (2014). *IRS Publication 15b (Fringe Benefits).* Available: http://www.irs.gov/publications/p15b/ar02.html. Last accessed 23rd Aug 2014.

Internal Revenue Service. (2014). *Publication 463 (2013), Travel, Entertainment, Gift, and Car Expenses.* Available: http://www.irs.gov/publications/p463/index.html. Last accessed 11th Aug 2014.

Internal Revenue Service. (2014). *Publication 54 Cat. No. 14999E Tax Guide for U.S. Citizens and Resident Aliens Abroad.* Available: http://www.irs.gov/pub/irs-pdf/p54.pdf. Last accessed 18th Aug 2014.

Internal Revenue Service. (2014). *Abusive Tax Shelters and Transactions.* Available: http://www.irs.gov/Businesses/Corporations/Abusive-Tax-Shelters -and-Transactions. Last accessed 12th Aug 2013.

Internal Revenue Service. (2014). *Recognized Abusive and Listed Transactions.* Available: http://www.irs.gov/Businesses/Corporations/Listed-Transactions-- -LB&I-Tier-I-Issues. Last accessed 12th Aug 2013.

Additional Resources

S-Corporation Defined:
Cornell University Law School. (2014). *26 U.S. Code § 1361 - S corporation defined.* Available: http://www.law.cornell.edu/uscode/text/26/1361. Last accessed 12th Aug 2013.

GSA Per Diem Rates:
U.S. General Services Administration. (2014). *Per Diem Rates.* Available: http://www.gsa.gov/portal/category/104711. Last accessed 14th Aug 2013.

International Agreements:
USA Social Security Administration. (2014). *U.S. International Social Security Agreements.* Available: http://www.ssa.gov/international/agreements_overview.html. Last accessed 15th Aug 2013.

USA Social Security Administration. (2014). *Status of Totalization Agreements.* Available:
http://www.ssa.gov/international/status.html. Last accessed 15th Aug 2013.

Tax Court Cases

UNITED STATES TAX COURT. (2010). *T.C. Memo. 2010-75.* Available:
http://www.ustaxcourt.gov/InOpHistoric/WILLOCKC.TCM.WPD.pdf. Last accessed 23rd Sept 2013.

UNITED STATES TAX COURT. (2014). *T.C. Summary Opinion 2014-74.* Available:
http://ustaxcourt.gov/InOpHistoric/MillerSummary.Guy.SUM.WPD.pdf. Last accessed 22rd Aug 2013

UNITED STATES COURT OF APPEALS FOR THE DISTRICT OF COLUMBIA CIRCUIT. (2000). *ASA INVESTERINGS PARTNERSHIP, ET AL., APPELLANTS v. COMMISSIONER OF INTERNAL REVENUE, APPELLEE No. 98-1583.* Available:
http://www.irs.gov/pub/irs-utl/asa_investerings.pdf. Last accessed 17th Aug 2013.

State Tax

Alabama:

State of Alabama Department of Revenue. (2014). *Alabama Department of Revenue.* Available:
http://revenue.alabama.gov/index.cfm. Last accessed 25th Aug 2014.

Alaska:

State of Alaska Department of Revenue. (2014). *Alaska Department of Revenue.* Available: http://www.revenue.state.ak.us/. Last accessed 25th Aug 2014.

State of Alaska . (2014). *Division of Corporations, Business and Professional Licensing.* Available: http://commerce.alaska.gov/dnn/cbpl/Home.aspx. Last accessed 26th Aug 2014.

Arizona:

Arizona Department of Revenue. (2014). *State of Arizona Department of Revenue.* Available: http://www.azdor.gov/Home.aspx. Last accessed 26th Aug 2014.

Arkansas:

Akansas Department of Finance and Administration. (2014). *Individual Income Tax .* Available: http://www.dfa.arkansas.gov/offices/incomeTax/individual/Pages/default.aspx. Last accessed 26th Aug 2014.

California:

State of California Franchise Tax Board. (2014). *State of California Franchise Tax Board.* Available: https://www.ftb.ca.gov/index.shtml . Last accessed 26th Aug 2014.

California Secretary of State. (2014). *Business Programs.* Available: http://www.sos.ca.gov/business/. Last accessed 26th Aug 2014.

Colorado:

State of Colorado. (2014). *Colorado Business Express.* Available: https://www.colorado.gov/apps/jboss/cbe//. Last accessed 24th Aug 2014.

Connecticut:

State of Connecticut. (2014). *Department of Revenue Services.*Available: http://www.ct.gov/drs/site/default.asp. Last accessed 16th Aug 2014.

State of Connecticut. (2014). *Connecticut Secretary of the State.*Available: http://www.ct.gov/drs/site/default.asp. Last accessed 16th Aug 2014.

Delaware:
State of Delaware. (2014). *DIVISION OF REVENUE.* Available: http://revenue.delaware.gov/. Last accessed 16th Aug 2014.

District of Columbia:

District of Columbia. (2014). *Office of the Chief Financial Officer.*Available: http://cfo.dc.gov/. Last accessed 16th Aug 2014.

Florida:
Florida Department of State. (2014). *Division of Corporations.*Available: http://www.sunbiz.org/. Last accessed 19th Aug 2014.

Georgia:

State of Georgia. (2014). *Secretary of State.* Available: http://sos.ga.gov/index.php/. Last accessed 19th Aug 2014.

State of Georgia. (2014). *Department of Revenue .* Available: https://etax.dor.ga.gov/. Last accessed 19th Aug 2014.

Hawaii:

State of Hawaii. (2014). *BUSINESS REGISTRATION (BREG).* Available: http://cca.hawaii.gov/breg//. Last accessed 19th Aug 2014.

State of Hawaii. (2014). *Department of Taxation.* Available: http://tax.hawaii.gov/. Last accessed 19th Aug 2014.

Idaho:

State of Idaho. (2014). *State Tax Commission.* Available: http://tax.idaho.gov/i-1132.cfm . Last accessed 21st Aug 2014.

State of Idaho. (2014). *Secretary of State.* Available: http://sos.idaho.gov/. Last accessed 21st Aug 2014.

Illinois:

State of Illinois. (2014). *Secretary of State.* Available: http://www.cyberdriveillinois.com/home.html. Last accessed 21st Aug 2014.

Indiana:

State of Indiana. (2014). *Indiana Department of Revenue.* Available: http://www.in.gov/dor/index.htm . Last accessed 21st Aug 2014.

State of Indiana. (2014). *Business Services Division.* Available: http://www.in.gov/sos/business/index.htm. Last accessed 21st Aug 2014.

Iowa:

State of Iowa. (2014). *For Businesses.* Available: http://www.iowa.gov/For_Businesses/Running%20a%20Business. Last accessed 23rd Aug 2014.

Kansas:

State of Kansas. (2014). *Office of the Secretary of State.* Available: https://www.kssos.org/. Last accessed 23rd Aug 2014.

Kentucky

State of Kentucky. (2014). *Kentucky One Stop Business Portal.*Available: http://revenue.ky.gov/. Last accessed 23rd Aug 2014.

Louisiana

State of Louisiana. (2014). *Louisiana Department of Revenue.*Available: http://www.rev.state.la.us/. Last accessed 23rd Aug 2014.

Maine:

State of Maine. (2014). *Maine Revenue Services.* Available: http://www.state.me.us/revenue/homepage.html. Last accessed 23rd Aug 2014.

Maryland:

Comptroller of Maryland. (2014). *Spotlight on Maryland Taxes.*
Available:
http://taxes.marylandtaxes.com/Business_Taxes/General_Informati
on/Business_Tax_Credits/. Last accessed 23rd Aug 2014.

Massachusetts:

State of Massachusetts. (2014). *The Official Website of the
Department of Revenue.* Available: http://www.mass.gov/dor/.
Last accessed 25th Aug 2014.

Michigan:

Michigan Taxes. (2014). *Department of Treasury.* Available:
http://www.michigan.gov/taxes. Last accessed 25th Aug 2014.

Minnesota:

Minnesota Revenue. (2014). *Welcome to the Minnesota
Department of Revenue .* Available:
http://www.revenue.state.mn.us/Pages/default.aspx. Last
accessed 25th Aug 2014.

Mississippi:

State of Mississippi. (2014). *Department of Revenue .* Available:
http://www.dor.ms.gov/. Last accessed 25th Aug 2014.

Missouri:

State of Missouri. (2014). *Department of Revenue .* Available:
http://www.dor.mo.gov/. Last accessed 24th Aug 2014.

Montana:

Montana.gov. (2014). *Welcome to the Montana Department of Revenue* . Available: http://revenue.mt.gov/. Last accessed 25th Aug 2014.

Nebraska:

State of Nebraska. (2014). *Secretary of State.* Available: http://www.sos.ne.gov/dyindex.html . Last accessed 25th Aug 2014.

State of Nebraska. (2014). *Department of Revenue* . Available: http://www.revenue.nebraska.gov/index.html . Last accessed 25th Aug 2014.

Nevada:

State of Nevada. (2014). *Secretary of State.* Available: http://nvsos.gov/. Last accessed 25th Aug 2014.

New Hampshire:

New Hampshire. (2014). *Department of Revenue Administration.*Available: http://www.revenue.nh.gov/. Last accessed 28th Aug 2014.

New Jersey:

State of New Jersey. (2014). *Division of Taxation.* Available: http://www.state.nj.us/treasury/taxation/index.shtml. Last accessed 28th Aug 2014.

New Mexico:

State of New Mexico. (2014). *Taxation & Revenue New Mexico.*Available: http://www.tax.newmexico.gov/. Last accessed 28th Aug 2014.

New York:

State of New York. (2014). *Department of Taxation and Finance.* Available: http://www.tax.ny.gov/. Last accessed 28th Aug 2014.

North Carolina:

State of North Carolina. (2014). *Department of Revenue.* Available: http://www.dor.state.nc.us/. Last accessed 29th Aug 2014.

North Dakota:

State of North Dakota. (2014). *Welcome to the official web site of the Office of State Tax Commissioner.* Available: http://www.nd.gov/tax/. Last accessed 29th Aug 2014.

Ohio:

Ohio Department of Taxation. (2014). *Commercial Activity Tax.*Available: http://www.tax.ohio.gov/commercial_activities.aspx. Last accessed 29th Aug 2014.

Oklahoma:

Oklahoma Tax Commission. (2014). *Oklahoma Tax Commission.*Available: http://www.tax.ok.gov/. Last accessed 29th Aug 2014.

Oregon:

Oregon.gov. (2014). *Department of Revenue.* Available: http://www.oregon.gov/dor/Pages/index.aspx. Last accessed 29th Aug 2014.

Pennsylvania:

Pennsylvania. (2014). *Department of Revenue .* Available: http://www.revenue.state.pa.us/. Last accessed 29th Aug 2014.

Rhode Island:

State of Rhode Island. (2014). *Department of Taxation.* Available: http://www.tax.state.ri.us/. Last accessed 29th Aug 2014.

South Carolina:
State of South Carolina. (2014). *Welcome to the South Carolina Department of Revenue.* Available: http://www.sctax.org/default.htm. Last accessed 29th Aug 2014.

South Dakota:

State of South Dakota. (2014). *Business Services.* Available: https://sdsos.gov/business-services/default.aspx. Last accessed 29th Aug 2014.

Tennessee:

State of Tennessee. (2014). *Department of Revenue .* Available: http://www.tn.gov/revenue/. Last accessed 29th Aug 2014.

Texas:

Texas Comptroller. (2014). *Window on State Government.* Available: http://www.window.state.tx.us/taxinfo/franchise/faq_tax_ent.htm l. Last accessed 29th Aug 2014.

Utah:

State of Utah. (2014). *Utah State Tax Commission.* Available: http://tax.utah.gov/. Last accessed 29th Aug 2014.

Vermont:

Vermont Department of Taxes. (2014). *Individual Income Tax Resource Area.* Available: http://www.state.vt.us/tax/index.shtml. Last accessed 29th Aug 2014.

Virginia:

Virginia Department of Taxation. (2014). *Virginia Department of Taxation.* Available: http://www.tax.virginia.gov/. Last accessed 29th Aug 2014.

Washington:

Department of Revenue Washington State. (2014). *BUSINESS & OCCUPATION TAX CLASSIFICATIONS.* Available: http://dor.wa.gov/Content/FindTaxesAndRates/BAndOTax/BandOr ates.aspx. Last accessed 30th Aug 2014.

West Virginia:

West Virginia. (2014). *State Tax Department.* Available: http://dor.wa.gov/Content/FindTaxesAndRates/BAndOTax/BandOr ates.aspxhttp://www.wva.state.wv.us/wvtax/WestVirginiaStateT axDepartment.aspx. Last accessed 29th Aug 2014.

Wisconsin:

Wisconsin Department of Revenue. (2014). *Wisconsin Department of Revenue.* Available: http://revenue.wi.gov/. Last accessed 29th Aug 2014.

Wyoming:

State of Wyoming. (2014). *Department of Revenue.* Available: http://revenue.wyo.gov/. Last accessed 29th Aug 2014.

Index

amended, 19, 115

amnesty, 115

amortization, 70, 98

AMT, 28-29, 127

Anguilla, 169

annuity, 175

apartments, 65

architecture, 107, 124

Arizona, 132-133

Arkansas, 133

assets, 28, 40-41, 45, 96-97, 113, 135, 143, 145-146, 150, 153, 159-160, 170, 174-176, 185, 187-188

assignments, 77

athletics, 107

auditors, 17

auto, 37, 59-61, 63

Bahamas, 169

bankruptcy, 112

bequests, 112

Bermuda, 169

bitcoins, 115

bonus, 66, 96-97, 133

meals, 77, 147

media, 59, 142

Medicare, 27, 83-84, 124

memberships, 68

mergers, 136

Michigan, 144

mileage, 37, 61-62

Minnesota, 144-145

Mississippi, 145

Missouri, 145-146

Montana, 146

motorcycles, 97

movies, 73

multinational, 173

municipalities, 152-153

musician, 74

Nebraska, 146

Netherlands, 168

Nevada, 36, 41, 147, 155

nonqualified, 86

Norway, 168

NY, 149

promotional, 72, 74

proprietorship, 37, 40

prorated, 70, 78

publications, 68, 79, 91

recapture, 66, 97, 103-104

redevelopment, 142

refund, 17, 19, 30, 118-119

refundable, 17, 118, 120-121, 123-124, 134, 138, 149

rehabbing, 125

reimbursed, 66, 165

reimbursement, 90

reincorporate, 42

reinvesting, 186

remodeling, 65

renewable, 127

renovating, 124

rental, 16, 18, 20, 72, 75, 93, 106-107, 144, 186

researchers, 126

residence, 42, 75, 113, 120, 125, 165

residency, 120, 169-170

restaurant, 71, 107, 147

retail, 51, 54

ABOUT THE AUTHOR

Not your average accountant by any means, Crystal was always the entrepreneurial type. As a teenager she read every book in the library on investment while living in a seventeen foot trailer, officially homeless, and working three jobs. Within a year she saved a down payment, leveraged through investing in stocks, and bought her first house at the age of 21. By 26 she was a millionaire, owning several businesses and a large real estate portfolio.

Crystal's interest in tax arose when nobody could say clearly how much tax she would owe when using various business or real estate investment strategies. This led to her pursuing an educational program for becoming an Enrolled Agent. After a few more years of work and study she found her answers; in the process becoming one of the most knowledgeable Enrolled Agents in the country with regards to investment and small business tax laws.

www.ingramcontent.com/pod-product-compliance
Lightning Source LLC
Chambersburg PA
CBHW072306210326
41519CB00057B/2814